# THE ☉ SUPERNATURAL

# THE ⊙ SUPERNATURAL

# Signs of Things to Come
## by Angus Hall

**ⅅ The Danbury Press**
A Division of Grolier Enterprises Inc.

Series Coordinator: John Mason
Design Director: Günter Radtke
Picture Editor: Peter Cook
Editor: Mitzi Bales
Research: Frances Vargo
General Consultant: Beppie Harrison

THE DANBURY PRESS
A DIVISION OF GROLIER ENTERPRISES INC.

PUBLISHER: **ROBERT B. CLARKE**

EDITORIAL CONSULTANTS:

**COLIN WILSON
URI GELLER**

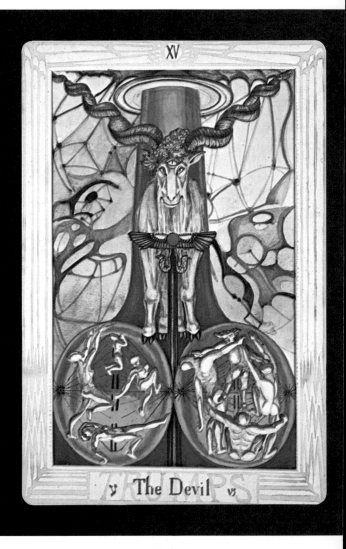

**Above: a Tarot card from the Aleister Crowley pack.
Frontispiece: the crystal gazer practices an old art.**

# Signs of Things to Come

We always want to know what tomorrow will bring. This book surveys the methods of looking into the future from *I Ching* to Tarot, from palmistry to crystal ball, and looks closely at the testimony of men and women — from Nostradamus to Jeane Dixon — who seem to have read the signs successfully.

# Contents

# 1

**The biggest ship in the world of its day, the new *Titanic* sank with great loss of life on its maiden voyage in 1912. Fourteen years before this tragic event, a novel uncannily foretold the occurrence.**

# The Future is Now

On a cold April night in 1898 the *S.S. Titan* —the largest, most luxurious, and above all, the safest ocean liner in the world—set out on her maiden voyage. She was ploughing the Atlantic between the English port of Southampton and New York when the unthinkable happened: she struck an iceberg, foundered, and sank. Most of her 2500 passengers were lost. This was not too surprising when it was realized that the 70,000-ton ship had only 24 lifeboats, capable of holding less than half those aboard. Even so, this

# "The most astounding instance of prophecy"

tragedy of giant proportions went unnoticed by the public in 1898. Why? Because the sinking occurred in a novel entitled *The Wreck of the Titan*, a story made up by a struggling and little-known English writer named Morgan Robertson. The book caused only a ripple at the time it was published.

Fourteen years later, however, Robertson's novel was belatedly hailed as a sensation, and described as "the most astounding instance of prophecy" of the 19th or 20th century. For, on the chilly night of April 14, 1912, the real 66,000-ton liner *Titanic* hit an iceberg and sank, with a calamitous loss of life. Like the fictional ship with such a similar name, the *Titanic* was on her maiden voyage across the Atlantic. Also like her fictional predecessor, she was a triple-screw vessel capable of a top speed of 25 knots. Both ships had a large number of passengers and crew, and far too few lifeboats for them—only 20 on the real one. Finally, both vessels were said to be unsinkable. One of the *Titan* deck hands in the book told a passenger that "God Himself could not sink the ship." With her 16 watertight compartments, the real ship *Titanic* was considered by her owners to take "first place among the big steamers of the world," and to be absolutely safe.

Almost as the *Titanic* went down, her survivors were already starting to talk of how the ship had been "doomed," and how they had felt all along that "something terrible" was going to happen. No one had forecast the catastrophe of the *Titanic* as accurately and vividly as the author Robertson had done in 1898, but there were some who later provided evidence of foretelling the tragic fate of the ship. Two seers who had been consulted by one of the passengers—the British journalist W. T. Stead—both said they had warned him against traveling on water in advance of his fatal journey. One of the fortune tellers had told Stead he would sail to America within a year or two from the time of the consultation. "I see more than a thousand people—yourself among them—struggling desperately in the water," he told Stead. "They are screaming for help, and fighting for their lives. But it does none of them any good—yourself included."

Stead himself had forewarnings of the ship's—and his own—unhappy end. Some years earlier, while editor of a London newspaper, he had published a fictitious account of the sinking of a huge ocean liner, supposedly written by a survivor. Stead added a prophetic editor's note to the story saying: "This is exactly what might take place, and what will take place, if liners are sent to sea short of boats." A few years after this, Stead wrote a magazine article in which he described the catastrophe of a liner colliding with an iceberg. Only one passenger in Stead's fictional article escaped with his life. Incredible as it seems, Stead also had a dream in which he saw himself standing on the deck of the sinking *Titanic*—without a life belt, and with the last lifeboat pulling away into the night.

Stead ignored all signs and omens of things to come, and lost his life on the *Titanic*. The case was different for a countryman of his, J. Connon Middleton. In a letter published in the journal of the Society of Psychical Research in London, Middleton recounted an "uncomfortable" dream which made him

Below: the 66,000-ton *Titanic* is here shown being towed out of port on the morning of April 10, 1912.

These two drawings of the big liner's end were based on eye-witness accounts given at the time.

Right: the great ship went down by the head. "She turned right on end," the third officer related.

Above: a heroic act ended the career of the *Titanic*'s captain, who lost his own life while saving a tiny baby passenger. One witness overheard the captain saying that he would follow after his ship.

Right: a contemporary photograph shows one of the *Titanic*'s lifeboats nearing rescue and safety.

"most depressed and even despondent." He had booked passage on the *Titanic* to attend a business conference in New York, he said. Ten days before the sailing date, he dreamed of the vessel "floating on the sea, keel upward, and her passengers and crew swimming around her." He had the same dream the following night, but this time, he told his wife, he seemed to be "floating in the air just above the wreck." Two days afterward, he received a cable that the conference had been postponed, and lost no time in canceling his booking. It was a lucky cancellation.

Colin Macdonald, a 34-year-old marine engineer, might also have died on the *Titanic*. However, he had a strong feeling of bad things to come for the big new ship. Three times he refused to sign on as the *Titanic*'s second engineer. In 1964 Macdonald's daughter was interviewed by a leading American psychical researcher and psychiatrist. She told him that her father had a "strong impression" that something was "going to happen" to

**Above: does time exist, or is it all in the mind? Do past, present, and future occur at the same moment, or are they strictly separate in experience? Such debates on time occupy the minds of philosophers as well as believers in the occult. As though to illustrate the debate, this painting by an unknown Elizabethan artist around 1596 shows the past, present, and future at one time in the form of Sir Henry Unton's life from his birth to his death.**

**Below: this 16th-century sundial deals fatalistically with the attempt to establish an exact point in time. It says: "Death is certain; only the hour is uncertain."**

the *Titanic*, and that there were also other times when he foresaw the future. The second engineer who took the *Titanic* job Macdonald turned down was drowned.

At the time of the *Titanic* disaster, 20th-century man was just beginning to question the prevailing materialistic philosophy that denied the unexplained. Precognition—that is, knowledge of future events by means outside the five senses—was viewed as freakishness or trickery. This was so whether the fore-knowledge came through dreams, palmistry, astrology, or simply a feeling that something—usually threatening—was about to happen. One scholar, cited by James Laver in his book *Nostradamus*, put it like this: "As the 19th century drew to its close, the rationalist and the materialist seemed to have established a permanent empire over thought. . . . [But] in times when the air is heavy with the sense of impending disaster . . . men find their rationalism shaken, and turn once more to the old superstitions which perhaps, after all, are not quite so

11

completely superstitious as 'advanced' people used to think."

The big debate was on the question of time. Ordinarily we use it as a measurement. In the simplest physical sense of the concept of time, we use it exactly like length, width, or volume. In this sense time does not exist independently. It is linear and ongoing, just as clocks and calendars are linear. But this concept of time does not take into account our intimate psychic relations with time past and time future, and ignores another time that we all experience—dream time. Taking these into account, it is possible to conceive of time as an entity in its own right—a psychic entity perhaps, but nonetheless real. If this was so, what was time's nature? Did time exist outwardly, or was it only in people's minds? Was it stationary or mobile? Was it strictly contained in separate capsules of past, present, and future, or did all three exist side by side at the same moment? This last notion was most passionately argued. There were those who believed that the future already exists, and that we approach coming events the same way as passengers on a train arrive at stations lying ahead of them along the line. Short of suicide, there was no way of intentionally avoiding these stations—and, it was argued, suicide itself could be the name of one of the stops ahead. In his book *What is Time?*, G. J. Whitrow relates how a Cambridge University philosopher used the death of the British queen in 1714 to give an example of the view that the future exists now. "At the last moment of time—if time has a last moment—it will still be the death of a Queen," the university professor stated. "And in every respect but one, it is equally devoid of change. But in one respect it does change. It was once an event in the far future. It became every moment an event in the nearer future. At last it was present. Then it became past, and will always remain past." This view agrees with what the American psychologist and philosopher William James called the "block universe," in which the future is like a strip of film whose pictures are revealed to us as the film unfolds.

A contrary view holds that people can affect their future by acting on warnings of things to come. This belief that man is not just a pawn to be maneuvered about and then finally sacrificed on the chessboard of the future, was restated in the late 1950s by the American novelist Jack Kerouac. He had one of his characters say: "Mankind will someday realize that we are actually in contact with the dead and with the other world—right now we could predict, if we only exerted enough mental will, what is going to happen within the next hundred years, and be able to take steps to avoid all kinds of catastrophes."

Strangely enough, it was neither philosopher or scientist who did most to analyze dreams, time, and visions of the future, and put them into a system. It was an aircraft designer, John William Dunne. His system was complicated and controversial, but not implausible. Dunne, who designed and built the first British military airplane, first became fascinated by "nighttime revelations of the future" in 1889 when he had an otherwise ordinary dream that foresaw the success of a Cape Town-to-Cairo expedition. From then on, he made a habit of writing down his dreams immediately on waking—or at whatever time

**Above: John William Dunne, one of the best-known time theorists, was not a man given to fancies. An aeronautics engineer who designed the first British military plane, he became interested in theories of time when he started to have clearly predictive dreams.**

Left: in one of his books, Dunne used this drawing to illustrate his theory of "the infinite regress." In it, an artist tries to paint a picture of the universe. Having started with the landscape before him, he realizes that he is missing from it. So he moves his easel back and paints himself in. Then he realizes that, to be right, the picture should have him painting himself. So he moves his easel back again—and goes on painting himself into the scene endlessly.

13

Whether simple or learned, people have always been concerned with time and telling time. This 16th-century German woodcut shows an untutored farmer reading the time from the shadow cast on his hand by a stick held under his thumb.

of day he recalled them—and then waiting for some element in the dreams to come true. His dreams were not at all unusual until 1916, when he had a "night vision" of an explosion in a London bomb factory. Such an explosion occurred in January 1917, with 73 workers killed, and more than a thousand injured.

By then, Dunne had come to the conclusion that he was "suffering, seemingly, from some extraordinary fault in my relation to reality, something so uniquely wrong that it compelled me to perceive . . . large blocks of . . . experience displaced from their proper position in Time." That realization, and the persistence of other clairvoyant dreams, led him to write his best-selling book, *An Experiment with Time*. He described the book as "the first scientific argument for human immortality." On its publication, he was flooded with letters from readers claiming to have had similar extrasensory experiences. This led him to note in the book's second edition: "It has been rather surprising to discover how many persons there are who, while willing to concede that we habitually observe events before they occur, suppose that such prevision may be treated as a minor logical difficulty, to be met by some trifling readjustment in one or another of our sciences or by the addition of a dash of transcendentalism to our metaphysics. It may well be emphasized that no tinkering or doctoring of that kind could avail in the smallest degree. If prevision be a fact, it is a fact which destroys absolutely the entire basis of all our past opinions of the universe."

In his book *Man and Time* J. B. Priestley devotes a whole chapter to Dunne. Although Priestley himself is best known as a novelist and playwright, he is also recognized as one of Dunne's chief interpreters. "Those of us who are Time-haunted owe him [Dunne] an enormous debt . . ." Priestley starts out.

It is to Dunne's work on dreams that Priestley gives greatest importance. Dunne, he said, established that ordinary dreams contain "a definite element of prevision or precognition." Following from this, Dunne effectively showed that the dreaming self cannot be entirely contained within time as we usually think of it. According to Dunne's time theory, we live in the flow of time as Observer 1 in Time 1. To the side of us is another self, Observer 2 in Time 2. From this, Priestley explains how Dunne's theory applies to seeing the future in dreams.

"What [Observer 2] observes are what Dunne calls 'the brain states' of Observer 1 (his experience in Time 1)—'the sensory phenomena, memory phenomena, and trains of associative thinking' belonging to ordinary waking life. Now when Observer 1 is awake, 2 is attending to what Observer 1 is discovering in Time 1, using the three-dimensional focus with which we are all familiar." [By this is meant the concept of ordinary time as flowing from the past through the present into the future.] Priestley goes on:

"But Observer 2 in Time 2 has a four-dimensional outlook. This means that the 'future' brain states of Observer 1 may be as open to Observer 2's inspection as 1's past brain states. But it also means that when Observer 1 is asleep, his three-dimensional focus can no longer act as a guide or 'traveling concentra-

Above: wooden "fan" calendars like the one shown here were used in medieval England. The 12 sides of the six strips corresponded to the months of the year, and holy days were clearly marked by pictures.
Right: this pillar, erected by the Mayans in 497, is like an almanac that covers five years. Predictions of future events are included.
Below: mechanical clocks came into being around the early 14th century. These handsome antique lantern clocks were made in England.

J. B. Priestley owes his fame to his novels and plays, but he is also well known as a disciple of time theorist John William Dunne. On a British television program in 1963, an appeal was made to viewers to write to him about any unusual time experiences they may have had. He is pictured here as he looks over the many hundreds of letters he received.

tion mark' for Observer 2. The latter is now left with his four-dimensional focus, which has a wide Time 1 range—much of it 'future' to Observer 1.

"But Observer 2 cannot attend and concentrate properly. Now and then he may succeed, as he must do in a clear pre-cognitive dream. Usually, however, unguided by the inactive sleeping Observer 1, Observer 2 with his four-dimensional focus is all at sea. . . .

"This relation between Time 1 and Time 2, between Observer 1 and Observer 2, enables Dunne to explain why we find most of our dreams so bewildering."

Priestley gives some examples of dreams that support Dunne's ideas of prevision. One of the most interesting is that of Dr. Louisa E. Rhine, who wrote about it herself in the American *Journal of Parapsychology*. She felt that the dream had helped her save the life of her one-year-old son. In her article she wrote: ". . . I had a dream early one morning. I thought the children and I had gone camping with some friends. We were camped in such a pretty little glade on the shores of the sound between two hills. It was wooded, and our tents were under the trees; I looked around and thought what a lovely spot it was." In the dream she decided to wash the baby's clothes and carried him with her down to the stream. She put him on the ground, went back to the tent to get the soap she had forgotten, and returned to find her son—who had been throwing pebbles into the water —lying face down in the stream, drowned.

She woke up "sobbing and crying," worried over the dream for a few days, and then forgot about it. It did not return to her until later that summer, when she and a group of friends went camping in a spot just like the one in her dream. She went to the stream to wash the baby's clothes, settled her son on the bank, and walked back for the missing soap. As she did so the infant picked up a handful of pebbles and began to toss them into the water. "Instantly," she stated, "my dream flashed into my mind. It was like a moving picture. He stood just as he had in my dream—white dress, yellow curls, shining sun. For a moment I almost collapsed. Then I caught him up and went back to the beach with my friends. When I composed myself, I told them about it. They just laughed and said I had imagined it. That is such a simple answer when one cannot give a good explanation. I am not given to imagining wild things." Such "displacement of time" can happen to anyone any night during sleep, and its frequent occurrence reinforced Priestley's faith in Dunne.

In the last part of his *Man and Time* chapter on Dunne, Priestley cites Dunne's strong belief that we are immortal. He interprets this part of Dunne's theory as follows:

"It is true that we 'die' in Time 1 when our Observer 1 reaches the end of his journey along the fourth dimension. And then all possibility of intervention and action in Time 1 comes to an end. This limits Observer 2's experience (through Observer 1's brain states) of Time 1, but it does not involve the death of Observer 2, who exists in Time 2. No longer having any Time 1 experience to attend to . . . Observer 2 now experiences Time 2 as Observer 1 did Time 1: that is, it is for him ordinary successive time as we know it. He has to begin learning all over again as his four-dimensional focus moves along the fifth dimension of Time 3. People and things will be the same and yet not the same. We catch glimpses, though confused and distorted, of this afterdeath mode of existence in our dreams.

"He [Dunne] suggests that in our Time 2 'afterlife,' once we have understood how to live it, we shall be able to blend, combine, build, with all the elements of our Time 1 existence, using them more or less as a composer does his notes, an artist his paints."

Priestley himself collected many stories about premonitions and other unusual time experiences. Among them was one reported to him by Sir Stephen King-Hall, a writer who was a naval officer for many years. Sir Stephen's story was as follows:

While on duty as officer of the watch on the *Southampton* in the war year of 1916, Sir Stephen had an overriding premonition that a man would fall overboard when the ship got to a small island off the coast of Scotland. His feeling grew stronger the nearer the convoy his ship led came to the island. With only his premonition to go on, Sir Stephen gave orders to the crew to get ready to save a man overboard. Of course, his orders were challenged by his superior officer.

". . . The Commodore said, 'What the hell do you think you are doing?' Sir Stephen recounted. "We were abreast the island. I had no answer. We were steaming at 20 knots and we passed the little island in a few seconds. Nothing happened!

"As I was struggling to say something, the cry went up 'man overboard' from the *Nottingham* (the next ship in the line, 100 yards behind us) then level with the island. Thirty seconds later 'man overboard' from the *Birmingham* (the third ship in the line, and then abreast the island). We went full speed astern; our sea boat was in the water almost at once and we picked up both men. I was then able to explain to a startled bridge why I had behaved as I had done."

In the 1930s, Air Marshal Sir Victor Goddard had a precognitive experience that seemed made to order for time theorists such as Dunne and Priestley.

While flying over Scotland during a storm, Sir Victor decided to descend in the area of the abandoned Drem airfield to get his bearings. He flew lower. When he was about a quarter of a mile away from Drem, something extraordinary happened: he found himself in both the present and the future.

"Suddenly the area was bathed in an ethereal light as though the sun were shining on a midsummer day," he said. The field was astir with activity as mechanics worked on biplanes in newly repaired hangars. Although Sir Victor was only 50 feet above the hangars, his plane went entirely unnoticed. He flew back into the storm and continued on his way.

What Sir Victor had seen came to pass four years later when Drem was rebuilt and reopened as a flying training school. "And then I knew that I had to sort out my ideas about free will and fate and determinism," Sir Victor declared.

In deciding this, Sir Victor was only one of the many divination converts who had gone before, and of the many more who were to come.

## A Flight Into The Future

Air Marshal Sir Victor Goddard was lost. Flying over Scotland in a Hawker Hart biplane, he was caught in a heavy storm. He needed a familiar landmark to get his bearings, and so flew lower to see if he could sight Drem, an abandoned airfield whose location he knew. He did sight it— but instead of the deserted and dark scene he expected, he saw a busy scene in bright sunlight (as shown by an artist's impression on the next page). Mechanics in blue overalls were hard at work on a group of yellow planes. He wondered that no one paid any attention to his low-flying plane, but, wondering, headed up into the clouds once more and went on toward his final destination.

That was in 1934 when Drem was indeed nothing but a ruin. In 1938, however, the airfield was reopened as an RAF flying school in the face of the war threat. Between these two dates, the color of British training planes was changed from silver to yellow —a fact that Sir Victor could not have known at the time of his strange experience. Thus, in 1938, anyone flying over Drem would have seen exactly what Sir Victor had seen four years before the event!

# 2

# Shamans and Other Sooth sayers

The young man had been behaving strangely for some days. First he had withdrawn into himself, shunning his friends and relatives and wandering off into the woods near his village. Then he had begun to sing, talk animatedly in his sleep, and experience visions that frightened those near him. Worse, however, was to come. After losing consciousness several times a day, he suddenly turned violent, and bodily threatened anyone who approached him. It was clear— especially to himself—that he could no

In early American Indian societies, the Shaman was one to be consulted and listened to—even by the Chief.

# "They crowded around for his words of wisdom"

Opposite: this drawing from a book published around 1810 shows the decorative ceremonial dress of a Tungus shaman from Siberia.

Above: a Lapp shaman lies in a trance in preparation for his fortune telling activities. His vital magic drum remains on his back. Below: a shaman of the Siberian tribe Karagass is robed in ornate dress trimmed with fur, feathers, and appliqués, and carries a drum.

longer remain in the community. Shouting abuse, he fled to the forest. There he remained, eating tree bark for food and drinking any water he could find. Occasionally he threw himself suicidally into a stream, wounded himself with his knife, or set fire to a branch and deliberately burned himself. He also caught and gnawed animals, and generally behaved wildly. A week passed in this manner. Then—bloodstained, filthy, and smelly—he returned to his home. There he was welcomed as a hero by his fellow villagers. They crowded around him, waiting to hear his words of wisdom and prophecies for the future. For the young man had passed his initiation tests, and was now a *shaman*—a magician–priest–doctor.

It took two more weeks before the new shaman was able to speak of his experiences, and to tell the people of his primitive central Asian village exactly what would befall them—whether they would prosper or fail, survive or go under in the years immediately ahead. Meanwhile, he continued to have periodic bouts of strange behavior and trances, during which it was believed he left his body and went to the realm of the dead to converse with the spirits there. From the spirits he learned what the likely fate of the community would be—which winters would be harsh and which mild, whether the herds of cattle would increase or perish, and, perhaps most significant of all, who the next shaman (or shamans) might be.

Shamans are good magicians as opposed to sorcerers, who are only interested in power and self-aggrandizement. They have been in existence for some 25,000 years, and are still to be found today in the Arctic and in Asia, particularly Siberia. To become a shaman involves more than just a cruel and self-harmful initiation. Before reaching this point, the candidate must have shown that he is worthy to undergo the tests. It is preferable if his nomination is hereditary, because everyone then expects him to behave as if possessed one day. However, there are various other ways someone can show that he is one of the chosen—one of those whose magical powers make them the most important and revered men in their tribe. It can be by an accident, such as falling from a tree or being touched by lightning; by feeling the call, much as a member of the Christian clergy gives himself to God; or by the simple expedient of a bold announcement that he is a shaman, and that he will prove it by bizarre and masochistic behavior.

In Lapland and Siberia, shamans would beat on their multicolored and many-imaged drums when calling up visions or seeking news of the future. The images—painted in reindeer blood or alder juice—represented the various gods of the wind, sun, and moon, as well as the spirits of humans and animals of the underworld. The shamans took their drums from special skin containers, and placed small brass rings on them. Then, tapping the drums with hammers, the shamans could see the future as the rings vibrated on the images. Ordinary Laplanders also used a drum as a fortune-telling device until the 18th century. No home was without its magic drum. The head of the household—wearing his best and newest clothes—consulted it on important domestic matters. However, when it came to issues that affected the whole community, it

Right: dolls were often a part of shaman rituals. This puppet with jointed limbs, used by Kwakiutl Indians of the Pacific northwest, symbolized the spirit that presided over shaman ceremonial dances.

Below: this small ivory doll was worn as a charm by Eskimo shamans during communication with spirits.

24

was left to the shamans to go into a self-induced trance, and to interpret the message of the drums.

There have been many debunkers of shamans. Some say that all of them are no more than deranged exhibitionists and frauds, and that their gifts of prophecy are restricted to finding lost or strayed dogs, cattle, or sheep. Others protest that the shaman's great powers of healing are no more potent than a quack doctor's, and that they fool themselves and their fellow tribesmen when they claim both to visit the dead and to guide the souls of the newly deceased to the other world.

One writer on Arctic shamans, agreeing with the view that they were disturbed personalities, stated: "The excessive cold, the long nights, the desert solitudes, shortage of vitamins, etc., took their toll of the nervous constitution of the Arctic populations, producing either mental illnesses . . . or the shamanic trance. The only difference between a shaman and an epileptic was that the latter could not bring about a trance at will."

Madmen or not, humbugs or otherwise, shamans are recognized as masters in transporting themselves and their followers into a state of ecstasy. It is true, too, that shamans have a far more extensive vocabulary than their co-villagers and, like the priests in the Middle Ages, use their superior knowledge to gain sway over the general group. As far as divination is concerned, their greater knowledge may enable them to convince their communities that they can see the future.

Another authority on shamans, who studied their role as prophets and healers among the tribes of the Sudan, believed that they were as balanced and normal as the rest of their tribesmen. "No shaman," he states, "is, in everyday life, an 'abnormal' individual, a neurotic, or a paranoiac; if he were, he would be classed as a lunatic, not respected as a priest . . . I recorded no case of a shaman whose professional hysteria deteriorated into serious mental disorders."

The controversy still surrounding the shamans is an indication of how fascinated mankind is with fortune tellers. Of course, there are many ways of foretelling the future besides shamanism. Some have long and colorful histories, which are still being added to by those who practice the prophesying arts today.

One of the oldest methods of soothsaying is the reading of sand, and, to several North American Indian tribes, this practice has a clearly magical quality. The Navahos in particular use colored sand in certain of their rites. Painting mystic pictures with colored sand is an ancient custom of theirs, and they believe that the legendary chief, Thunderbird, was sent down from the sky especially to instruct them in the making and interpretation of sand pictures. By trickling sand through their fingers, the tribal wise men made patterns on the ground. These patterns revealed how someone should act in a given situation, whether or not a sick person would get well, and how to solve difficult and worrying problems. The pictures—which only the medicine men could correctly interpret—had to be erased before the sun sank. If they were left for anyone to see after that, it was believed that they not only would lose their magic, but also that evil men could study them, and perhaps

## Magic for the Hunt

The hunt was all-important to the Cro-Magnon community of more than 12,000 years ago. Failure meant hunger, and, perhaps, death. The hunters were skilled and had weapons —but even braves ones quailed at the thought of the danger. However, the hunters got magical aid from the shaman, their magician-priest, who performed a ritual for a successful hunt. He might burn clay models of animals to represent their killing, for example, but whatever he did, he enacted man's mastery as a way of making it come true.

European cave paintings of the period 28,000–10,000 B.C. often depict a creature part man and part animal, as below. Many scholars think these are shamans in dress of skins and headpieces.

Above: the Navaho medicine man, like other shamans, is a healer as well as a fortune teller. He begins a ritual cure by painting a greatly symbolic design on sand.

Above right: around the finished sand painting are prayer sticks, rattles, and the colorings used.

learn Thunderbird's secrets of the sand to put to evil use.

Sand paintings are essential to the Navaho healing ceremonies, which are done today in the traditional way of long ago. The medicine man creates one or more paintings with colored sand on the ground. He may set others to help work on the designs because their complexity often requires many hours of labor. The sand pictures, properly called "dry paintings," are often elaborate and always symbolic. The patient must sit within the main sand painting during the long ceremony, which in some cases can last for several days. At the very beginning of the ritual cure, some of the sand from the painting is rubbed on the sick person's body. This is done to draw the spirits' attention directly to the patient and his or her illness.

Today, reading sand pictures can be a party game that adds a little spice of magic to the fun. Whoever is chosen to act as seer is blindfolded, and given both a tray containing fine dry sand and a pencil. The *querant*—that is, the person seeking information—sits quietly near the sand diviner, concentrating on the question he or she has asked. The seer holds a pencil in his hand, with his wrist resting on the rim of the tray. By the time three to five minutes have passed, and provided that both the querant and the fortune teller have cleared their minds of everything but the question, the pencil should move as of its own accord. Initials, if not words, will appear in the sand. A "y" will stand for yes, an "n" for no, an "m" for maybe, and a "p" for perhaps. Instead of letters or words, lines may be formed—a long deep one tells of a journey, and a short deep one announces an unexpected visitor, for example. In still another way, shapes may be drawn on the sand. A triangle stands for a successful career; a small circle for a coming marriage; a large circle for misfortune near at hand; a cross for a hazard to face or obstacle to overcome; an X, or "kiss" cross, for a love affair—happy if the cross is distinct, unhappy if it is indistinct. The width of the tray is gauged as a year, so time can be measured by dividing the sand into halves, quarters, or twelfths. Thus, questions about when the bad luck will pass, or when a romance will start, can be answered.

The time of a future event cannot be told in like manner by another widespread and ancient form of prediction—dice. Palamades is said to have invented dice in Greece about 1244

**Right:** the sand painter scatters corn to call upon the help of the spirits in bringing about a cure.

**Below:** as the sick child sits on the sand painting, the medicine man chants his ritual invocation.

**Right:** shamans of Madagascar use sacred seeds to foretell the future. They drop the seeds into circles drawn on the ground, and find the answers to questions in the patterns the fallen seeds form.

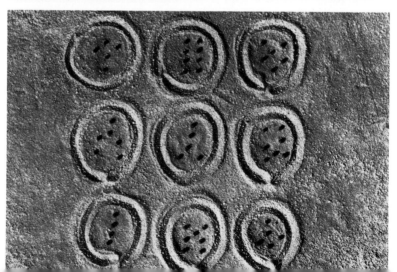

B.C., but there is evidence of their use before that. In earlier Egyptian civilizations, bone-like ivory molds—called *astragals*—were thrown to see what future events they revealed.

To consult the dice, a person tosses them inside a chalk circle drawn on a board or table. If one or any of the dice roll outside the circle, they are not included in the calculations—but this foretells a quarrel. If they fall to the floor on the toss, an estrangement is in the offing. The system is speedy and simple, although interpretations vary. Some say *three* means a pleasant surprise; *six*, the loss of something of value; *nine*, a wedding; *twelve*, an important letter on the way; *fifteen*, a warning of danger; *eighteen*, extreme good fortune. It is considered unwise to throw dice on a Monday or a Wednesday.

A most unusual novel of 1971, *The Dice Man* by Luke Rhinehart, is about divination by dice. In it, the leading character decides his every move by the throw of the dice, for which he sets all his own readings of the numbers. Thus he rampages through New York committing rape (his interpretation of *one*), murder (his reading of *three*) and other misdeeds.

People who are fascinated by numbers, as thousands are, may be inclined to choose the centuries-old system of reading dominoes to tell them of happenings to come. In the Western way of reading dominoes, all blanks are removed, and the remainder spread face downward on a table. All *ones* refer to travel, *twos* to social affairs, *threes* to romance, *fours* to finance, *fives* to work, and *sixes* to good luck. Using their left hands, two people alternately draw three pieces each. The two numbers on each domino are then read together. A *six* and a *one*, for example, means a fortunate voyage; a double *three* indicates an especially happy marriage; and a double *four*, a large windfall. The two pieces that no one wants to draw are the *three-one*, which foretells bad news, and the *four-two*, a sign that a disappointment is due. The Eastern Method of reading dominoes is somewhat more complicated. It employs the full domino set, and has 27 different and fuller meanings. It is thought to be unlucky to consult the dominoes more than once every seven days.

Reading pictures from the fire, or *pyromancy*, is the most personal of all the many different forms of divination. The formations of the coals project such different pictures and images to each person that it becomes impossible to tell any fortune but your own. To get the best results from the flames—and the clearest pictures—it is necessary to have a lively, roaring fire. This can be produced by throwing salt or sugar onto coals that may have burned down. Settled before the fire, you start by gazing into the flames for five minutes or so. If during this scene setting a piece of coal should leap out of the grate and land at your feet, the next 12 months will bring good luck and happiness.

The pictures do not necessarily have to be of shoes (which foretell of good news coming reasonably soon), or hatchets (meaning that disaster looms ahead), or anything as distinctive as that. Large circles or rings indicate a happy marriage, and double rings a hasty marriage that may fail. A shape like a

**Right: when people say "the die is cast," they probably don't know that they are referring to dice-throwing as an ancient form of fortune telling. (Die is the singular of dice). The Greeks of antiquity are said to have invented dice to help reveal the future. By the time of this 4th-century B.C. terra cotta statue, however, playing dice was more of a gambling game. Even so, the winner was the player who got the most favorable omen from the dice.**

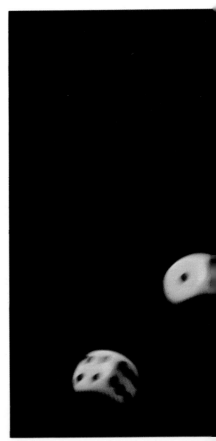

Right: this South African witch doctor casts and reads the "wise stones" to see what the future might reveal for his tribe.

Below: playing dice is almost purely a form of gambling today, but the old idea of consulting them is not entirely lost. This is done more as a way of making a decision than as a method of seeing into the future, however.

Who will I marry? This question has given rise to many customs involved with trying to see one's future spouse—especially if the questioner is an unmarried woman. Above: in American lore, the unwed girl who looks into her mirror at midnight on Hallowe'en while holding a lit candle will, it is said, see the image of her husband-to-be peering at her reflection over her left shoulder.

Right: another old American practice made a kind of party game out of trying to get advance news of a marriage partner. Young men and women peeled an apple or potato without breaking the peel, tossed it over their shoulders, and read the letter the fallen peel most closely resembled. The letter was supposed to be the initial of the future spouse.

Above: in old England, maidens in love placed nuts among the hot embers of the hearth, and whispered their loved one's name. If the nut jumped, it meant that the love affair would be successful.

Above: in another English custom, a small piece of wedding cake was passed through a wedding ring, and put under the pillow. This was supposed to bring a dream of the man the dreamer would marry. Below: a modern novelty piece tells fortunes according to which finger a person wears a ring on.

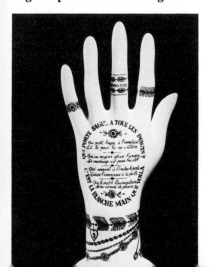

three-leafed clover denotes the greatest prosperity, well-being, and success.

The language of the flames is almost identical to that of tea leaves. It depends much on personal interpretation. The tea leaf reader takes the cup in her left hand, and swirls the dregs and tea leaves in a counterclockwise direction three to seven times. If a man is giving the reading, he swirls the leaves clockwise. Next she or her querant gently turns the cup over onto a saucer, and on turning it up again, checks to see if any drops remain in the cup. If they do, they foretell the probability of tears in the next few days. This is a better sign than no liquid at all, however. The mass of dark leaves alone bodes trouble and sorrow.

By using her intuition and imagination, the reader will interpret the numbers and initials she will be able to see in the leaves. To obtain the most positive reading, it is best to use a plain cup rather than a patterned one, which can divert the mind. Always keep the handle pointing south, and remember that the bottom of the cup represents the distant future, the middle of the cup means time not too far away, and the upper part of the cup stands for immediacy.

The art of reading tea leaves is often passed on from generation to generation, but it can easily be self-taught, and the basic rules are quickly learned. The shapes most frequently formed are those of serpents, birds, and animals. A snake stands for evil and temptation, a mouse for financial insecurity, and a rat for danger. A horse is a symbol of a lover, especially to women, and a goat tells of enemies and misfortune, especially to a sailor. A spider is a lucky sign, and when surrounded by dots, means great wealth. A hen speaks of an addition to the family, and a peacock promises an addition of property.

Other shapes that form in tea leaves, and their meanings, include a hammer (triumph over adversity), a ladder (travel), scissors (a fight), a steeple (disappointments), an umbrella (trouble and annoyance), an apple (long life), and an acorn (good or improved health). Every so often, the face or hands of a clock appear in the leaves. While most of the hours that might be shown have no constant meaning, 7:00 or 9:00 implies that there will be a death in the family, and midnight signifies a secret and profitable rendezvous.

Arlene Dahl, actress and beauty expert, tells this anecdote about reading tea leaves. It happened while she was making a film in England a few years ago. "I came across a book that explained all the symbols to look for in the bottom of the tea cup," she says. "At first I took the book along to parties, but every time I had to check out something, I could feel I was losing my audience—so I started to improvise. But I was right too often and I got scared." It was while in London that her new "talent" got her labeled as a witch. "My hairdresser insisted that I read her fortune," she goes on. "Although I didn't know it, she and her husband had wanted a child for five years, and when I read a new arrival she was overjoyed. A few weeks later she ran in and called me a witch—she was pregnant!"

Staying on the domestic scene for divination methods, it is

Above: ancient Rome had official augurs, such as the one depicted above on the fresco of a tomb. These augurs judged whether the gods approved or disapproved of planned actions by bird cries and flight, lightning, thunder, and other designated omens.

Above: some augurs read the signs by allowing birds to eat grains placed on the letters of the Greek alphabet, drawn on a circle. Words were formed from the letters left without grains, and the words thus formed gave the answer that was sought.

possible to make a stab at telling the future with knives. All that is needed is an ordinary table knife and a round tray big enough to hold it. The tray is marked around the rim with various brief prophecies, which can be written on slips of gummed paper and stuck in place. Each person twirls the knife by its center three times — women using their right hands, and men their left. The message at which the blade points after the third twirl is the fortune. If the knife stops in a space between messages, this suggests that the coming days or weeks will be relatively uneventful. Nowadays divination by knives is a light-hearted game, but it was previously practiced in a more serious way by North American Indians.

Another common household implement that has long been a tool for telling fortunes is the mirror, the use of which goes back to the Iron Age. The so-called "magic of the mirror" was known both to the early Chinese sages and to the wise men and prophets of Greece, all of whom considered it an omen of death to dream of seeing your own reflection in water, copper, glass, or any other shiny surface. Extending this to waking hours, it was felt that gazing at one's reflection in water was forbidden by the "spirits of the lake." These spirits would, in fact, drag the gazer's soul down into the depths, and leave the physical body to die on the bank. The threat of a watery grave if one defied the water spirits was carried over as a threat if one gazed at oneself too much in any reflecting surface. Yet men and women defied the threat in the early practice of *hydromancy,* divination by water. They read their future fate by peering at their reflections in water. If the image was clear and remained undisturbed, it was an omen of serene and hopeful days to come. If the image was broken or got ruffled, it foretold of trouble—and perhaps even death. The idea of seeing into the future by studying reflections was later transferred to the use of mirrors.

The Egyptians, Greeks, and Romans spent a significant amount of their waking moments peering into bronze and silver mirrors, hoping to see pictures of the future. At the beginning of the 13th century, glass mirrors were first introduced in Venice, and then the art of mirror divination, or *catoptromancy,* thrived. The mirrors used were often handsomely encased. They were dipped into water to see whether a subject's reflection would show good or ill fortune. When the special ornate mirrors were not available, substitutes could include anything with the power to reflect—from polished stones to fingernails.

Health matters could be foretold by the mirrors, and it was not uncommon for them to be used to show the whereabouts of missing treasures or people, and the fate of nobles, leaders, and kings. In Europe in the Middle Ages, mirrors were used as a positive deterrent against wickedness, being said to protect their owners from the baleful influence of the Evil Eye. Among the Chinese of former times, small mirrors were placed about the house to frighten off evil spirits, which were thought to be terrified at the sight of their own reflections. For the young girls of old, however, mirrors had a more romantic and optimistic purpose: they were employed to reveal at what moment in the future love would come.

It was customary throughout Europe for a maiden to examine

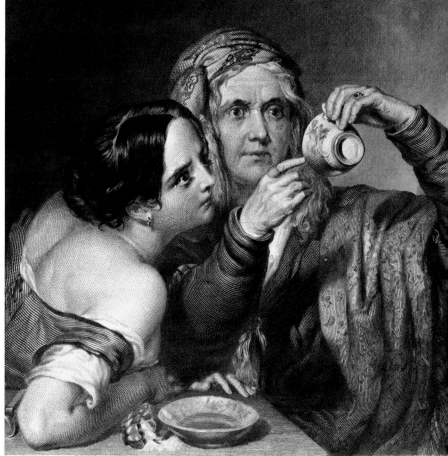

Above: this African witch doctor will read fortunes from the marks left by a crab scrambling about in a bowl containing wet sand.
Right: because of the vagueness of the shapes formed by tea leaves, a good tea leaf reader has to depend a great deal on intuition, skill, and sensitivity.
Below: Moroccan girls at turn of century had such a strong belief in kites as an omen of the future that if theirs broke—which meant bad luck—they were plunged into a deep depression.

the moon's reflection in her hand mirror to see how many years would have to pass before her wedding day. The years were calculated mainly by the length of time that passed before clouds obscured the moon, or a bird flew across it. In the USA it was said that if a girl—especially a virgin—looked into a mirror at midnight on Hallowe'en, the reflection of her husband-to-be would be revealed over her left shoulder.

Maidens also had other sources for predictions about love and marriage. In the English county of Oxfordshire, it was long held that if a girl put an ivy leaf in her purse or pocket, she would marry the first man she met—even if she already had a husband. When a girl wanted to discover if her lover was faithful to her, she had only to place two nuts together on the bars of a grate. If they burned as one, her beloved was constant and true. However, if the nuts were forced apart by the heat, she would know beyond doubt that her man was faithless. In the North of England a willow wand was used as a magic guide to finding a husband. Holding the wand in her left hand, an unmarried girl had only to leave her house secretly, and run three times around it while she said: "He that's to be my good man come and grip the end of it." At the completion of the third lap, a likeness of her future mate would appear, and catch hold of the other end of the wand.

The list of ways humans have sought to learn the future ahead of time is by no means exhausted. Throughout the world and the ages, peoples have tried divination by *belomancy* (arrows), *ornithomancy* (flight of birds), *sortilege* or *cleromancy* (drawing

This Blackfoot Indian medicine man, dressed for a healing ceremony, wears the mask of the particular evil spirit thought to have caused the illness. It was believed that with the right mask, the shaman could speak directly to the offending spirit and persuade it to go away.

or casting of lots), and *ceromancy* (candle wax drippings). A notorious example of present-day use of sortilege is among the Mafia, whose members sometimes draw lots to decide who will kill a person who has tricked or betrayed them. However, of the ancient arts of prognostication, ceromancy is probably the one in most ominous use today. It has particular association with voodoo. Voodoo priests read candle wax drippings to advise others how to improve their love life, increase their money, or bring about the downfall of their enemies. Voodoo candle readings can last up to 12 hours, usually from 6 p.m. until dawn. During this time, wax drippings are allowed to fall into a shallow dish of cold water, and the patterns they form are interpreted by the priest or seer. If necessary, spells are cast. There are shops in New York City that sell wax figures to be used as fetishes for sticking pins into. Although the candles, wax figures, and dishes are on open sale, the all-important incantations that go with using them are not. No practicing Voodoo priest would ever sell or barter them. In this, he is like the shaman who opened this chapter: his art is a secret and personal art.

An example of the shaman's power became part of American Indian folklore in 1811. Tecumseh, the chief medicine man of the Shawnees, was greatly displeased when some 5000 Creeks refused to join his campaign to stem the US government's conquest of Indian lands. "You do not believe the Great Spirit has sent me. You shall know," he is quoted as saying. "I shall stamp my foot and the earth will tremble." This prophecy was realized two months later. On December 16, 1811, Tecumseh stamped his foot—and the first of three shocks tore through some 50,000 square miles of territory, including where the offending Creeks lived. Indians called it "the greatest earthquake in the history of man." It has been cited as an awesome example of the power of the shaman—who can not only foresee the future but, in some cases, make it come about through what magic no one else knows.

Although today the shamans of Asia are reportedly losing their prophetic strength and their ability to engineer events, this does not appear to be the case among the American Indians. In 1962, a group of Indians were arrested for fishing near the Trinity River in northern California, and their relatives foretold of a "Great Killer Windstorm" that would strike the Pacific Northwest because of this. On Columbus Day of that year, a fierce storm in that region killed 50 people. Three years later, in November 1965, came the great electricity failure that blacked out the Northeast coast and turned New York into a city of darkness. The blackout was ascribed to the magical powers of the Indians by at least one person—Craig Carpenter, the tall, hawk-faced man active in the current, highly militant Indian Rights movement. "What everybody seems to forget about the Northeast's blackout," he states, "is that it started in a power relay station on land stolen from the Tuscarora Indians; and nobody yet has figured out *how* it started."

The following year, a drought hit Washington, D.C. Throughout the long, hot summer, the residents yearned for rain. Finally, a 107-year-old Hopi, Chief Dan Kachongva, was consulted. Through his interpreter, Thomas Banyacya, he said: "It will rain, don't worry." That night the rain started—and did not stop until 24 hours later, just as the interpreter had also predicted.

Not content with that demonstration of divination, Banyacya and other Indians marched on Niagara Falls in 1966. They said that the Great Spirit would reveal His powers there to show that when they told of an event in the future, they spoke the truth.

The Indians congregated at the Falls on September 17, 1966 —New York State's official annual Indian Day. The following morning a front page story in *The Washington Post* said: "A flaming meteorite lit up the skies across the north central United States last night, frightening hundreds of persons who saw it before it broke up in bits of smoking debris over northern Indiana . . . Michigan Governor George Romney, flying in his private plane . . . said 'the meteorite almost hit us. It really frightened us—we thought we were under attack. All of a sudden the thing was coming and it was as bright as noon.'"

To most people it seemed incredible that Banyacya—or anyone—could have known that such a thing was about to happen. However, to those who had knowledge of the shamans, who understood and appreciated their powers of divination, and who accepted that such powers could be handed down, there was nothing extraordinary about the event. It was simply another indication that the future can be ours for the making— or, at least, for the predicting.

Was the New York blackout of 1965 satisfactorily explained by the scientists? American Indians strongly suggest that their magical powers were the cause of it. Below: stranded commuters slept where they could, as this flash photo shows. How many would believe in a supernatural cause?

# 3

# Ancient Arts of Fortune Telling

Confucius—the Chinese wise man and philosopher whose teachings helped shape his country's entire civilization—was almost 70 when, in 481 B.C. he stated, "if some years were added to my life, I would give 50 to the study of the *I Ching*, and might then escape falling into great errors." At the time, Confucius had already worn out three pairs of leather thongs that bound the tablets on which his copy of the world's "most revered system of fortune telling" was inscribed. As it turned out, he had only

# "Symbolism with hidden and puzzling meanings"

two more years to live instead of 50, but he spent them in deep and exhaustive study of the meanings and mystery of the *I Ching*, known as the *Book of Change*. This book, he said, had "as many layers as the earth itself." Hundreds of years later, when the Samurai warrior class ruled Japan, it was said that Samurai planned military strategy by consulting *I Ching*—which they continued right up to the 19th century.

No one can be sure of how old the *I Ching* (pronounced EE Jing) is, but it is believed to date from 2852 B.C. as the work of the legendary Emperor Fu-hsi. The contents of the book were systemized by King Wen in 1143 B.C., and his work was further clarified by his son, the Duke of Chou. Still later, Confucius edited and added explanatory notes to the *I Ching*. For all of this, the *Book of Change* remains full of symbolism with hidden and puzzling meanings.

The book contains 64 hexagrams shown by combinations of six solid and/or broken lines, as, for example:

Each hexagram symbolizes a specific human characteristic or condition of life, which is reflected in the symbolic name it bears. For example, hexagram 1 is "creative"; 11 is "peace"; 20 is "contemplation"; 37 is "the family"; 46 is "ascending"; 55 is "prosperity"; and 64 is "before completion." These hexagrams are formed by two sets of three lines, called trigrams, each of which also have their own name. The trigrams affect the reading of the *I Ching* by their own special qualities, images, and position—whether at the top or bottom of the hexagram.

It was King Wen who formulated the 64 hexagrams, gave them their names, and put the text message with them from the original work of Fu-hsi. After King Wen's death, his son Chou added notes to help explain the meanings of individual lines of the hexagrams, and the overall symbolism of them. The West owes its knowledge of *I Ching* to James Legge, a 19th-century specialist in Chinese studies. He translated the *Book of Change* into English in 1854, and his is the only thorough, scholarly translation of the entire book in English.

One of the most important things to remember about *I Ching* is that it is a whole system of philosophy. It is based on a code that embodies the traditional moral and mystical beliefs of the Chinese. Therefore, a querant cannot go frivolously to the *Book of Change*. Nor will he or she get an easy, direct "yes" or "no" answer. Questioners are thrown back on themselves for the interpretation of the answers, which are intended only as a guideline. As Raymond Van Over says in his edited version of *I Ching*: "It directs the questioner's attention to alternatives and the probable consequences of our actions if we choose one path instead of another. If the oracle wishes to direct our action in a specific direction or through a particular channel, it will tell us how a Superior Man would conduct himself. In this subtle

One of China's greatest philosophers and scholars, Confucius was deeply interested in the mysteries of the *I Ching*. He thought it worthy of 50 years of study.

**Right: modern Korean followers of Confucius hold a procession on the philosopher's birthday.**

**Below: this 19th-century engraving shows someone about to throw the yarrow stalks that will lead him to the parts of the *I Ching* he must read to learn about his fate.**

Left: it is simpler and just as effective to use coins instead of yarrow stalks to consult the *I Ching*. The coins shown here are Chinese bronze ones of old design, but any kind will serve.

Below: these sample hexagrams from the *I Ching* show the complexity, symbolism, and hidden meanings of the ancient text.

## LÜ

**10 TREADING CAREFULLY**

Lü suggests the idea of one treading on the tail of a tiger which doesn't bite him. There will be progress and success. Hazardous position — no distress or failure.

## TA YU

**14 ABUNDANCE**

Ta Yu indicates that there will be great progress and success. The superior man represses evil and gives distinction to what is good.

## KUAN

**20 CONTEMPLATION**

Kuan intimates he should be like the worshipper who has made his ablutions, but not yet his offering. With sincerity and dignity he inspires trust and respect.

way, our actions are directed toward a positive goal while still allowing us the free will to choose our own ultimate destiny. We can, of course, decide not to act as the Superior Man, and take any course we choose.''

With the question in mind, there are two ways of consulting the *I Ching*: one by tossing three coins of any kind, and the other by throwing 50 yarrow stalks in a given sequence. The second method is long and complicated, and, since there is no proof that it gets any different results, can be left to the strict traditionalist or purist. Therefore, let us see how using the coins works.

The tossing of the coins reveals which hexagram the querant should consult as applicable in his case. A toss turning up two tails and one head is written as a solid line, ——————. A toss of two heads and one tail is written as a broken line, —— ——. Three tails are written ——x—— and three heads, ——o——. There are six tosses, and the first toss becomes the *bottom* line of the first trigram. Each succeeding toss is written as a line *above* the other until all six lines are drawn. Then, the questioner refers to a chart that gives him the name of the hexagram so indicated. Complications come in with what are called ''moving lines''—three heads or three tails—which can refer the questioner to more than one hexagram. However, these do not always come up. In some cases, one or more individual lines of the hexagram are read as well as the text, commentary, and additional notes. In other cases, only the text is read. The coin toss says what to do in the way it forms the hexagram. In no case will the advice be immediately clear, for each hexagram has layer upon layer of meaning.

It has been said of the *I Ching* that, over the centuries, some 3000 scholars have tried to unravel its mysteries. This indicates

**Above: this sidewalk fortune teller of Japan holds the *I Ching* yarrow stalks in readiness. He generally combines astrology and palmistry for making forecasts.**

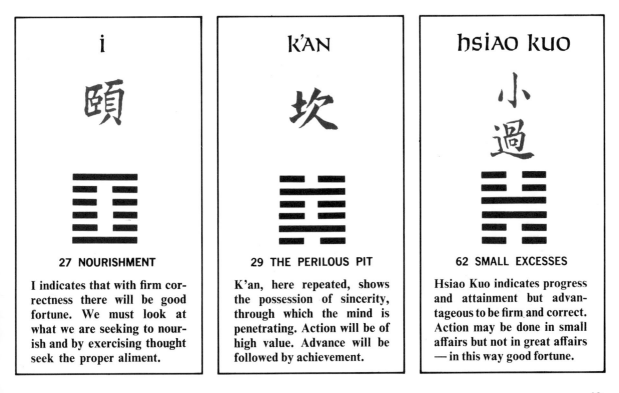

## i

頤

**27 NOURISHMENT**

I indicates that with firm correctness there will be good fortune. We must look at what we are seeking to nourish and by exercising thought seek the proper aliment.

## K'AN

坎

**29 THE PERILOUS PIT**

K'an, here repeated, shows the possession of sincerity, through which the mind is penetrating. Action will be of high value. Advance will be followed by achievement.

## hsiao kuo

小過

**62 SMALL EXCESSES**

Hsiao Kuo indicates progress and attainment but advantageous to be firm and correct. Action may be done in small affairs but not in great affairs — in this way good fortune.

43

that the book can hardly be regarded as just a fortune-telling system—more complicated and venerable than the horoscopes in our daily newspapers, perhaps, but no more important or valid than they are. When the book is studied for its ideas and ideals more than its prophetic properties, it can open the way to an understanding and finer appreciation of the universe's unceasing evolution and movement.

The more intuition used by the questioner of *I Ching*, the greater will be the range of choice open to him—for the book aims not to tell the future as such, but to determine whether or not the questioner is acting in accordance with his best interests. More than that, it can relate the individual's best interest to the wider world—even the universe. In fact, to become the Superior Man—which is one of the book's ideals—the questioner must necessarily follow the Right Path. He can only do this when he considers the fate and fortune of his fellow human beings.

Those who consult the *Book of Change*, either for themselves or as an interpreter for others, should look after their copy of the book with veneration and care—even if it is merely a paperback. When not in use, it should be wrapped in a piece of good clean cloth and placed on a shelf high enough that no one can look down on it. Just before using it, a person should wash his hands thoroughly in respect for the book. That done, he should place the *I Ching* facing south on a table in the center of the room and burn incense on another table that's lower. The seeker should prostrate himself three times on the floor while facing north. Only then, according to the strictest rules, is he ready to ask his question.

In the hexagram answers, the lines are based on opposites—starting with solid and broken for the drawing of the lines themselves. The solid lines stand for what is positive, light, active—all embodied in the Yang. The broken lines stand for the opposite of these: negative, dark, passive—the Yin. In Chinese philosophy, Yang stands for the hard, outgoing approach to life; Yin for the soft, shaded outlook. These two primary cosmic forces are like the two sides of a coin—one cannot exist without the other. Further, though they are in opposition to each other, they are also interdependent.

One of the most famous hexagrams in the *I Ching* is 4, entitled "youthful inexperience" or "youthful folly," which looks like this:

Anyone whose coin tosses refer him to this hexagram will discover that he is in need of a "proper direction." He is told that his immaturity and folly is the result of "uncultivated growth" and that he has rushed to the "foot of a mountain" where lies a "dangerous abyss." However, the *I Ching* goes on to say: "Yet such rashness may bring good fortune—fortune to be utilized when the moment comes . . . It is our sacred duty to

Above: thousands of years ago, Babylonian priests developed the reading of animal livers as a means of foretelling the future. This clay model of a sheep's liver is covered with symbols relating to possible future events, divided into 55 sections. It dates from between 1800-1500 B.C.

Below: the Assyrians used this kind of an instrument to make their astrological calculations.

Left: this 2nd-century Roman sculpture shows the casting of a horoscope. In this case, the subject is a tiny child. His future is being read by two women who are examining the celestial globe.

Below: the Romans, too, believed that they could learn about the future from the internal organs of animals. In this ancient stone sculpture, the augur consults the entrails of a bull.

Right: the Temple of Apollo in Delphi housed the most important oracle of ancient Greece, known as Pythia. Only the wealthy could afford the fees of the oracle, who also limited her appearances to given times. Yet many questions of state were decided by what the Delphic oracle foretold.

Above: proof that the high and mighty went humbly to the oracle at Delphi is found in this 5th-century B.C. Greek bowl. It depicts King Aegeus of Athens listening to the words of Pythia.

correct the follies of youth through education." This can be interpreted to mean that the questioner has reached a given stage in his life, which is bound up with the universal situation. What the seeker must do is to decide whether he will advance or retreat, whether he will continue just as before, or alter his actions so that his course is not so rapid, so dramatic, so impulsive.

Whatever the questioner does, the decision—and the responsibility for that decision—are totally his. From this it might seem that the *Book of Change* is as remote and unfeeling as a recorded message on the other end of the telephone. However, this point of view is both an oversimplification and a misreading. The *I Ching* offers the advice of a wiser and older friend who looks at the problem broadly rather than from one person's narrow self-interest. In his updated version of the *Book of Change*, John Blofeld stresses the fact that the *I Ching* is unique because, in place of "rigid prophecies" it makes suggestions "based on an analysis of the interplay of universal forces, not about what *will* happen but what *should* be done to accord with or to avoid a given happening."

The *Book of Change* indicates that a man must not fight against the whirlpool when he is cast into it, but must *move with it* to survive. By continuing in what the *I Ching* calls the "course of righteous persistence"—one that harms no one and is in the public good—a person will eventually find his reward in this life rather than the next.

People's search for something to put them in touch with the rhythm and nature of the universe was in progress long before the *I Ching* was written. More than 5000 years ago in Mesopotamia, men and women sought signs of the future above their heads in the stars, or beneath their hands in the intestines of dead animals. Astrology was born in the Mesopotamian city of Babylon. Living in secluded monasteries near especially built high towers, Babylonian priests discovered five other planets besides the Earth, Sun, and Moon. Without the aid of telescopes, but with the blessing of unusually clear and cloudless skies, they succeeded in plotting the "workings of the heavenly spheres." These they related to the plagues, fires, earthquakes, and famines that beset the world. They asserted that everything was subject to the same set of celestial laws, and they drew up the first zodiac based on universal application of such laws.

Left: this is how the supreme oracle of Delphi looked in the imagination of the 19th-century English artist Sir Edward Burne-Jones. The painting, which hangs in the Manchester Art Gallery, shows the oracle in front of the sacred flame. In her hands she holds the bay leaves that are the emblem of her priestly position.

This zodiac was split into twelve parts in accordance with the number of lunar cycles in a year. Astrology replaced to some degree the Babylonian fortune-telling method called *hepatoscopy*, or inspection of the liver. According to the Babylonians, the liver of a man or a sheep was the "seat of life," and the coils and turns of a sheep's entrails contained messages about the future. The priests made clay models and tablets of livers and intestines, and said that these were the "prophetic books" of the gods.

Although astrology grew rapidly in popularity, hepatoscopy stayed in fashion until around 2000 B.C. At that time, reading the future from the liver lost favor because of the deduction by scholars that the heart was the true seat of life.

Astrology went from Babylonia to China and the Far East by way of the well-traveled smugglers' route of ancient days. However, the Chinese used a different set of stars and terms, and, instead of the zodiac, developed the Lo King. The Lo King is in the form of a disc on which there are six circles. These show the stars, the planets, and groups of other symbols. Providing the exact hour of birth was known, the disc could tell a person everything that would happen to him on earth and in the world to come. Besides being helpful to a ruler during his reign, the disc was invaluable in deciding exactly when he should be buried in order to flourish in afterlife. Marco Polo, the Venetian who spent many years in China during the 13th century, wrote of the Lo King: "I observed that when a Prince or great leader died, the magic disc was consulted as to whether the planets which governed his birth were in the ascendant. If they were, he would be buried without delay. If they were not, it was no uncommon thing for the corpse to remain unburied for up to six months before it was finally cremated or put in the ground. It all depended on the heavens and what they told."

The Greeks showed an interest in the stars later than the Chinese and the Babylonian innovators. For many years, the

48

Above: this fantastic depiction
of the universe was done in 16th-
century Germany in the form of
a woodcut. In it, a person has
crawled through the rim of the
universe, and has discovered the
control mechanism for the stars.

favored method of fortune telling in Greece was *cleromancy,* or
divination by drawing lots. This simple system was widespread
and important—even the all-wise oracle at Delphi was known
to have a supply of beans used as lots. In seeking a glimpse of
his future by cleromancy, an ancient Greek had to ask only
questions that could be answered "yes" or "no". He would
write this question on a strip of lead, which was then put into a
jar containing black and white beans. The strip of lead was
drawn out together with a bean, and the question on the strip
was answered yes or no according to the color of the bean that
accompanied it.

In their great desire to look into the future—a trait that
seems to be common to humanity throughout history—the
ancient Greeks grew dissatisfied with the simple system of lots,
and developed the more sophisticated oracles. The oracles
spoke only from certain temples throughout the country, the
one at Delphi being supreme. They limited their appearance to
once a month, and charged an extremely high fee for their
services. Yet their influence was great, because they were often
consulted by political leaders on questions of state.

The oracle was usually a young woman of common rank,
said to have powers of prophecy and, therefore, known as a
sibyl. The all-important sibyl at Delphi was called Pythia. In
giving her prophecies, the oracle went into a trance during
which she was the medium for messages from the gods—
principally Apollo. Her answers were so garbled and riddle-like
that they had to be interpreted by a priest. This added to the
mystery and solemnity of the occasion. Later, when Pythia
spoke directly, some of her magic seemed lost.

The rising influence of consecutive philosophers such as
Pythagoras, Plato and Aristotle helped swing the Greeks away
from the oracles and toward astrology. Aristotle, who was an
avid student of astrology, declared that the earth was governed
by the motions of a "far superior world."

## He Predicted the Fire of London

"Having found, Sir, that the City of London should be sadly afflicted with a great plague, and not long after with an exorbitant fire, I framed these two hieroglyphics . . . which in effect have proved very true." So spoke William Lilly, a 17th-century astrologer, suspected of intrigue in the Great Fire of London by a government inquiry committee in 1666. One of the astrologer's "hieroglyphics" of prophecy is shown below. It is a drawing of Gemini, the sign of the City of London, falling into flames, and it was done 15 years before the fire that destroyed most of London. According to Lilly's report about the Parliamentary committee, he was released with "great civility."

To later Christians, there was a particularly striking instance of astrological power in the pages of the New Testament: it was a brightly shining star that led the three wise men to the newborn Jesus. The star they followed belonged to a constellation now known as Cassiopeia—the Woman and Child—from the Greek. Babylonians knew this constellation to preside over Palestine and Syria. Babylonian astrologers had also observed that the most prominent star of the constellation could only be seen once every 300 years—and then only when a future king had been born in Palestine.

From the Christian era on, astrology established itself among the main methods of fortune telling. One of the first big attacks against it came around the beginning of the 18th century from the caustic pen of satirist Jonathan Swift. Known for his biting comment against all he disliked, Swift was particularly opposed to "the bogus art of star-reading." In 1707, an almanac writer known as "Partridge" published his predictions for the year, and Swift was wildly incensed by Partridge's warning against the "outpourings of imposters."

Taking up his pen and, according to a colleague, "dipping it in vitriol," Swift quickly composed his own *Predictions for the year 1708, by Isaac Bickerstaff. Written to prevent the people of England from being further imposed on by vulgar Almanack Makers.* After supposedly studying the heavens, Bickerstaff (Swift) came out with some startling prophecies, including the imminent death of Partridge. "I have consulted the star of his nativity by my own rules," claimed Swift, "and find that he will infallibly die upon the 29th of March next, about 11 at night, of a raging fever." The fact that Partridge was still alive on March 30 was of no consequence to the "all-knowing, all-seeing" Swift. Again as Bickerstaff, he produced another pamphlet, *An Account of the death of Mr. Partridge, the Almanack Maker, upon the 29th instant, in a letter from a Revenue Officer to a Person of Honour.*

To no avail did Partridge write or give denials of his death. He was stopped in the street by straight-faced wits who asked to be reimbursed for money they had contributed toward his coffin. An official of his parish church sent him a number of notes requesting that he "be a good fellow and come and be buried with the rest of the dead." The publishers of his almanac, the Stationers' Company, did him the worst injury of all: they marked him in their ledgers as "deceased," and refused to accept any further commissions from him! It was seven years before the unfortunate Partridge was able to get his predictions printed again. By then, astrology itself had taken several near-fatal blows from scientists and thinkers of the Age of Enlightenment.

**Right: astrology was put into the shadow by the "age of reason" of the 18th century, but it still was not without some loyal followers. Ebenezer Silby, an English doctor who described himself as an "astro-philosopher," published a vast volume on astrology entitled *The Celestial Science of Astrology*. In it appeared this illustration of the horoscope he had cast for King Louis XVI and Queen Marie-Antoinette. In telling how he foresaw their doom in their stars, he said: ". . . the stars in their courses fought against this illustrious pair."**

Lewis 16th King of France
Born 23 Augt. 3 H 30 Ms.
P.M.
1754.

Marie Antoinette Queen of France
Born 2 Novr. 7 H 23 Ms.
P.M.
1755.

Crown'd
11 June
1775.

Lewis Capet Executed 21 Jan.
10 H 20 Ms. in the Morning
1793.

Marie Antoinette of Lorrain & Austria
Widow of Lewis Capet
Executed 16 Octr. 11 H.
30 Ms. in the Morning
1793.

The decline in astrology continued with the discovery in 1781 of a new planet, first called Georgium Sidue and later named Uranus. For many people, this discovery made a mockery of the astrologers' centuries-old system that, naturally, excluded Uranus. Scholars, too, went back to the famous *Confessions* of St. Augustine (A.D. 354–430), in which he explained why he had lost faith in astrologers. He said that the very different fates of twins, especially identical twins, and of a rich landowner and his slave who had both been born at precisely the same time, made him question the truth of astrological prediction. "No art at all is involved in soothsaying," he declared, "and only accident makes some of its predictions come true."

By the start of the 19th century, however, astrology appeared to be like Mr. Partridge—it was said to be dead, but it refused to be buried. The revival of interest in the stars and their meanings began in England with the publication in 1819 of James Wilson's *A Complete Dictionary of Astrology*. Eight years later, Robert Cross Smith's periodical *The Prophetic Messenger* started to appear. Known as "the father of modern astrology," Smith wrote and edited under the name "Raphael." On his death in 1823, leadership went to his chief disciple with orders that the name Raphael be kept alive forever. Today, *Raphael's Almanac, Prophetic Messenger, and Weather Guide* is still being published.

It was not until the late 1920s and early 1930s that astrology again became respectable on both sides of the Atlantic. In 1926, the founder of the College of Astrology in San Francisco formed the National Astrological Association—now known as the American Federation of Astrologers, with headquarters in Washington. In 1930, the London *Sunday Express* increased sales by running the astrological predictions of R. H. Naylor. In the fall of that year, Naylor spectacularly forecast the crash of the dirigible R-101, "the greatest airship ever built." Other professional astrologers followed Naylor into print. During the war years of 1941 in England, the *New Statesman* magazine of August announced that: "Today more people follow their fate (or Hitler's) in the stars, as interpreted by the astrologers, than follow the day-to-day news of God (or Satan) as outlined by his archbishops and vicars." Today, in the United States alone, some 2000 newspapers carry astrology columns, and more than 7500 astrologers enjoy an affluent present from their work on the future. Every so often, one of them makes a daring and seemingly impossible forecast. This was the case with Charles Jayne who, in 1948, predicted that "no-hope" President Harry Truman would win over Thomas E. Dewey. Jayne was right, the skeptics were wrong—and once again astrology held its own.

As ever, Confucius had one of the first—and probably one of the last—words on the subject of fortune telling. He considered that predictions based on the planets were more than just possible. They were necessary if individuals were to be shown the error of their ways in advance as a way to check and change themselves for their own good, and for the benefit of others. "Heaven sends down its good or evil symbols," he wrote in one of his explanatory notes to the symbolic and philosophical *I Ching*, "and wise men act accordingly."

Left: a modern day astrologer, Ingrid Lind is connected with an astrological center in London. She believes that good astrologers are also psychologists, but are not prophets.

Left: the many commercial astrologers of New York City vie for business. Here one advertises by means of a sandwich man.

Right: what could be more modern than a horoscope reading by computer? Here is one that spews out nearly 23 feet of fortune telling information about health, career, and personal problems. It also gives the personal lucky number of those who have consulted it.

# 4

# What the Body Tells

**Right:** phrenology enjoyed a great vogue in Europe and America in the 19th century, and was the most popular of all the psychic arts at one point. Early prenologists classified the bumps on the head into 26 divisions, and read character according to how well or how poorly the bumps were developed. For example, a large bulge at the area marked 1 on this chart would signify a sensual nature, and an underdeveloped one would mean coldness. This detailed phrenological chart is of a period when 40 classifications were listed.

**Below:** Mir Bashir is a successful palmist of the present day, having a much-visited consulting room in a fashionable part of London. He offers help in many areas of human problems, and considers himself a specialist in vocational guidance and marriage counseling.

On a bright sunny morning in July 1894, the palmist Cheiro—whose clients were to include King Edward VII of England, the humorist and writer Mark Twain, the spy Mata Hari, and the film stars Lillian Gish and Mary Pickford—strode briskly through London's Whitehall on his way to the War Office. He had been summoned there by one of the most renowned soldiers in the British Army, Horatio Kitchener. Cheiro passed through the gloomy but imposing entrance, and was directed to a large, mahogany-

LANGUAGE
35

55

# "Your life is at great risk"

paneled office on the first floor. There Kitchener stood nervously waiting, his hands clasped behind his back. He showed Cheiro to a chair, and, after a few moments of casual conversation, he leaned forward abruptly. He paused, fingered his full moustache, and said haltingly: "I want you to tell me about my future. There's something worrying me and I don't know what it is. Do you think you could put my mind at rest"?

By observing Kitchener's physique and bearing, and by noting his inability to remain still, Cheiro had already decided that here was a man of limitless courage and determination. But this man was also in danger of being undermined by something he probably loathed to believe in—Fate. The palmist then asked his client to put out his right hand, the one by which the future could be foretold. After studying it for some minutes, Cheiro raised his head and said quietly: "I can see nothing but success and honors for you in the next two decades. You will become one of the most illustrious men in the land, in the world indeed. But after that your life is at great risk. I see a disaster at sea taking place in your 66th year. It does not, however, mean that you will necessarily die. If you do not travel on water in the year 1916, you will live to reap even more fame and riches."

At the time, Kitchener was aged 44, and, as Cheiro predicted,

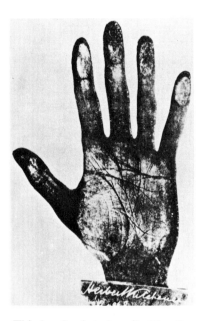

This hand print, described by the expert palmist Cheiro as showing an artistic bent, belonged to military leader Lord Kitchener—who, in fact, was an ardent student of literature, languages, and music. However, the lines also indicate the level-headedness and practicality that must have contributed to his army career. The impression was made in 1894 when Lord Kitchener, at the age of 44, was already widely known.

Right: Lord Kitchener was one of those drowned when the armored cruiser *Hampshire* was sunk by German mines in World War I. Cheiro had predicted this untimely end in the 1894 reading.

his major military achievements lay ahead of him. Four years later he captured Khartum. Then he distinguished himself in South Africa against the Boers. Then, at the outbreak of World War I, he was appointed Britain's War Minister. In 1916—and now Lord Kitchener—he was invited to visit Russia by the Czar to discuss Russia's role against Germany. Ignoring Cheiro's warning, and thinking only of the Allied cause, the minister sailed from a naval base in the North of Scotland, bound for the Russian port of Archangel. The cruiser carrying him—the *H.M.S. Hampshire*—was still in British waters when, at 7:40 p.m. on June 5, she struck a German mine and went down with the loss of most of her hands. Kitchener, who was in the gunroom when the explosion sounded, disappeared into the Atlantic. His body was never found. Later, Cheiro gave his own account of his interview with the dead Field Marshal, stating: "The Line of Life gave the expectation of a long life under ordinary conditions, but my prediction . . . was based on the cross at the end of the travel line opposite the age of 66."

Cheiro, who was born Count Louis Hamon in Ireland in 1866, and took his name from the Greek word *cheir*—meaning hand—is still considered one of the leading authorities on palmistry. In making his reading for Kitchener, Cheiro followed

Above: Lord Kitchener had been warned not to travel by sea in his 66th year—when he drowned.

1    2    3    4

## What Shape is Your Hand?

These drawings appear in Cheiro's book *You and Your Hand* to illustrate the seven types of hands.

**1** *The elementary hand* is short and thick, with stubby fingers and heavy palm. It indicates a slow thinker of stolid nature who is guided by his instincts.

**2** *The square hand* is just that— clearly square in palm, base of fingers, and fingertips. It tells of a person who is level-headed, and very good in business.

**3** *The philosophic hand* is long and angular with pronounced joints on long fingers. This type of hand denotes the deep thinker who may be hard to understand, and who is sensitive and dignified.

**4** *The spatulate hand* has broad, flat fingertips, and a palm that is much broader at one end—either at the wrist or under the fingers. It points to energy, unconventionality, inventiveness, and love of action. Its possessor will be independent and original in anything he or she undertakes to do.

**5** *The conic or artistic hand* is full and well shaped, either conic or round and with rounded, tapering fingers. Those with this hand love all things artistic, even if they are not creators of art. They are good conversationalists, at ease with strangers, and generous in money matters.

the time-honored and basic rules of palmistry—which must be applied whether the reading is given in a tent, an office, or the privacy of one's home. He asked Kitchener no personal questions, but quickly turned to studying the client's right hand. (The left hand gives signs of a sitter's disposition and character.) Before examining the lines, however, he categorized the whole hand as one of seven main classes created by the French palmist Casimir D'Arpentigny: (1) elementary hands, with the short thumb and short thick fingers that indicate a manual worker rather than a thinker; (2) square hands, medium size and with strong well-developed fingers that speak of practicality, precision, moderation, and perseverance; (3) philosophical hands, with large thumb and palm, and knotty finger joints which reveal someone decisive and unemotional, who prefers reason to faith, logic to idealism, and who criticizes himself before others; (4) spatulate hands, shaped like a spade and with flat fingers, which show that the person is optimistic, self-confident, intelligent, and likely to rise to the top; (5) artistic hands that are pliable and have a delicate thumb and long tapering fingers, such as point to the poet, the artist, the musician; (6) psychic hands, the outward sign of a "dreamy" person who loves beauty, and who would rather go to a lunchtime concert than spend the money on lunch itself; (7) mixed hands, with fingers of different shapes, which bother the professional palmist, and confound the amateur.

Kitchener had mixed hands. The fact that he held them behind his back told Cheiro something else about the soldier: he was a cautious man who would painstakingly investigate a person or a situation before coming to any conclusion or decision. Had the soldier clasped his hands in front of him, it would have denoted dignity, calmness, and a slow-moving serenity. The most forbidding pose of all is when a subject lets his or her left hand dangle at the side, with the right hand level with the waistline, the palm uppermost, and the fingers partly clenched. Here is someone bloated with his own importance, who expects obedience and deference, and who feels that his opinions and wishes are the only ones that count.

After noting how a person holds his hands, Cheiro—or any budding palmist—would note the color of the hands, the texture of the skin, and the "feel" of the flesh. Pink and red

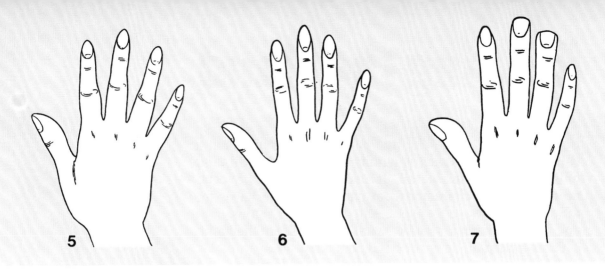

5         6         7

hands tell of good health and energy. White hands are the opposite of this, while yellowish or sallow hands proclaim suspicion, irritability, bitterness, and the "blues." You don't need to be a Sherlock Holmes to realize that fine skin goes with refined natures, and that rough coarse skin points to the reverse. A palm that feels soft and offers no resistance belongs to someone who drifts uncaringly through life, and a palm that is firm reveals that its owner has a mature and rewarding balance between energy and rest. A hard palm that has no elasticity when pressed goes with the finger-clenching egotist—though when both traits are present, the indication is that the person may have boundless resource and drive, but no proper direction. The length of fingers is also of significance, as is the shape of the nails (see diagram on this page). For example, long nails go with even-tempered people who are slow to anger; short nails with fault-finders and those fond of arguments; oval nails with those who feel sorry for themselves and have little push; round nails with those having fiery but usually short-lived passions; and square nails with disciplinarians and lovers of order.

It was the thumb, however, that most impressed Cheiro and his fellow palmists. "Know the thumb and you know the man," they said. They point out that, while the lines a person is born with are like so many finely traced roads along which a person will travel, it is the thumb that acts as the signpost. The fingers are no more than milestones along the path of life. Whatever qualities, characteristics, talents, inclinations, or skills someone has, it is the thumb that tells whether or not he or she will put them to full or only partial use. The thumb also tells whether an individual is likely to rush toward the danger that may await him, or if he will be more prudent, less hasty, and so avoid or minimize the lurking threat. Generally, the larger the thumb and the heavier its tip, the better it is for its owner. It is even

**6** *The psychic hand* is long and slender, with tapering fingers and pointed tips. Its possessor is gentle, idealistic, and too easily deceived or imposed upon. It points to an unworldly person who is easily influenced and hurt.

**7** *The mixed hand* has fingers from different types of hands, and no clearly classifiable shape. It shows great adaptability to work, people, and circumstances, but a lack of fixed purpose. One with this hand believes deeply in luck.

Below: the shape of the nail is an indicator of health. According to Cheiro, long wide nails (A, B) warn of lung weakness, and long narrow ones (C) of spinal weakness and general delicacy. Short nails of rounded shape (D, E, F) show a tendency for laryngitis, bronchitis, and general throat and nose ailments. Short broad nails (G, H, I,) indicate bad circulation and heart trouble. Shell-shaped nails (J, K, L) point toward possibilities of paralysis.

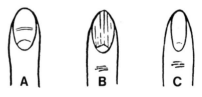

A     B     C

D    E    F    G    H    I    J    K    L

# Reading the Hand

Look at your hands. The line patterns, the mounds and valleys, the shape – each is wholly individual to you, and unlike anyone else's at all. It takes years of study and practice to read character from hands – and, perhaps, see the future. However, anyone can follow the major lines and features to get an idea of what you can see in the hand. This simplified guide is for beginners.

**The Mount of Venus: if full and well-rounded, denotes abundant physical energy in addition to strong sexuality.**

**The Plain of Mars: once said to point to a quarrelsome nature, this area is given less importance in readings now.**

**The Bracelets: three clear lines fore-tell health, wealth, and happiness; chained ones mean a life of hard work.**

**The Mount of the Moon: if well-developed, shows a mystical turn of mind; if flat, it can indicate instability.**

**The Line of Intuition: points to intuitiveness. If present, and if strong, may denote possible psychic abilities.**

**The Life Line:** shows physical vitality and pattern of life rather than length of life. A long, strong line indicates balance and stability; a chained or weak line can point to indecisiveness.

**The Fate Line:** indicates state of personality balance. Not on all hands, but if there, a strong line denotes a well-developed ego; a weak or broken line can mean a tendency to self-doubt.

**The Heart Line:** tells about emotions. A straight line points to strong independence; a line curving toward the index fingers shows a loving nature; a drooping line can mean insecurity.

**The Head Line:** shows intellectual and career tendencies. A straight, clear, and even line denotes practicality and reasoning powers. A gracefully curved one indicates an imaginative nature.

**Finger of Jupiter (index):** a long one means success; one shorter than the third finger may mean insecurity.

**Finger of Saturn (middle):** a long one denotes coldness; a short one is said to mean an intuitive, creative nature.

**Finger of Apollo (ring):** a long one may mean deep introversion; a crooked one is believed by some palmists to show a tendency to get heart disease.

**The Sun Line, also called Line of Apollo:** shows creative energies. A strong line means ability to do great things.

**Finger of Mercury (little):** if set apart from the others, it could mean difficulty in human relationships, and also in sexual and financial matters.

more auspicious if the thumb joins the hand low instead of high. Thus, small thin-tipped thumbs set high on the hand are likely to be possessed by those who are lacking leadership, judgment, and will power, and whose uncontrollable emotions will lead them into trouble, misery, and pain.

When Cheiro was at the peak of his influence and fame, he was the first to admit and emphasize that the art of palmistry was one of the most contradictory ways of forecasting the future. "Just as no two painters use exactly the same technique, so no two palmists use the same methods, or even come to the same conclusions," he said. "I wrote my first book on palmistry when I was 12, and since then I have been astounded—if not dismayed—by the many ways in which both my predecessors and my contemporaries—to say nothing of my successors—have differed from me both in working methods and in interpreting what is contained in the hand."

Apart from a reading made directly—which, ideally, should take place in a comfortable and relaxed atmosphere with good light—it is possible to make an imprint of a person's hand, and take it away for further study. Cheiro—who had a collection of 60,000 such prints—did this in the case of Lord Kitchener, bringing with him to the War Office some sheets of glossy paper, a rubber pad, a tube of fingerprint ink, and a roller of the type used by photographers. In making the hand print, the palmist pressed the hand firmly down so as to show fingers, thumb, palm, and "bracelets"—the three lines running across the wrists, which are favorable omens if clearly marked, and otherwise if not. He took prints of both hands.

Professionally, Cheiro was extremely fortunate. He was aware of this, and often told friends that, had he been practicing at certain times in the past, he would have been arrested and accused of "trafficking with the Devil." His knowledge of the history of *chirognomy* (the telling of character from hands) and *chiromancy* (foretelling the future from hands) was extensive. In his research, he traced the related arts back to 1000 B.C., when mention of palmistry was made in the Vedic writings of ancient India. He also studied one of the "elevated and inquiring" books that the philosopher Aristotle wrote for his pupil Alexander, later Alexander the Great. According to the philosopher, it was based on an Arabic treatise he found "graven in letters of gold, upon an altar dedicated to Hermes [the messenger of the Gods]." The oldest palmistry manuscript known in England was the *Digby Roll IV,* dating back to 1440, and the first book to be published in Europe came some 35 years later with Johan Hartlieb's *Die Kunst Ciromantia (The Art of Chiromancy)*, printed in Augsburg after his death.

In the last decades of the 14th century, an Italian named Andreas Corvus made a name and a fortune for himself as a "practical palmist." He caused a sensation by his warning that a certain citizen of his native Bologna would commit a "detestable murder" on September 24, 1504. The prophecy came true when that very person—either to oblige or out of malice—struck and killed Corvus himself on the day in question. An equally bizarre fate befell the palmist Tibertus Antiochus, who took Corvus's place. He predicted the violent·

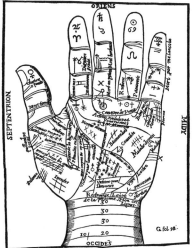

Above: this diagram of the hand for reading its lines was created by Jean Belot, who was a palmist in 17th-century France. His system gave a nod to astrology, too, for he related the zodiac and the planets to different areas of the hand. Belot, like other early palmists, paid a great deal of attention to lines that would be considered unimportant nowadays.

**Above: since their appearance in Europe—probably about the 14th century—gypsies have been known for their fortune-telling skills. This early 17th-century painting shows a gentleman having his palm read. Below right: modern gypsies still practice palmistry as a way of earning money. Here they ply their traditional trade in Camargue, France.**

death of a military adviser called Guerra. When asked how he himself would die, he answered: "It has been decreed from all eternity that I shall end my days on the scaffold." Sure enough, Guerra was stabbed to death by someone, and Antiochus, falsely accused of the crime, was sentenced to be hanged. Thus his prediction came true.

These macabre happenings led many people to keep their hands to themselves, and out of the way of palmists. A series of attacks was launched on those who made easy money—and made people uneasy—by reading palms, and wandering bands of gypsies were soon in the front line of fire. In 1530, King Henry VIII of England acted against "an outlandish people calling themselves Egyptians . . . who have come into this realm, and gone from shire to shire in great companies, and used great subtle and crafty means to deceive people, bearing them in hand that they, by palmistry, could tell men's and women's fortune, and so many times, by craft and subtlety, have deceived the people of their money and have also committed many heinous felonies and robberies." James I, when he came to the throne a century later, added his venom against the "devil-dealers." In 1664, the English writer Richard Saunders warned his readers

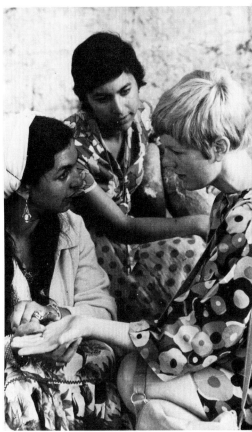

against palmists in London, stating, "(there) lurk in obscure corners, in and about this famous city, many illiterated pieces of nonsense and impudence . . ."

The odium in which palmists were held spread to France. There they were condemned by the Church, and it was stated that, "now no man professeth publicly this cheating art, but thieves, rogues, and beggarly rascals." Despite this, however, it was in France in the mid-18th century that the palmist Johann K. Lavater was most popular. A clergyman from Zurich, Lavater was also a *physiognomist*—one who reads character from faces. He anticipated the forensic science of fingerprinting when he announced that "the hands of man are equally diverse and dissimilar as their faces . . . just as it is impossible to find

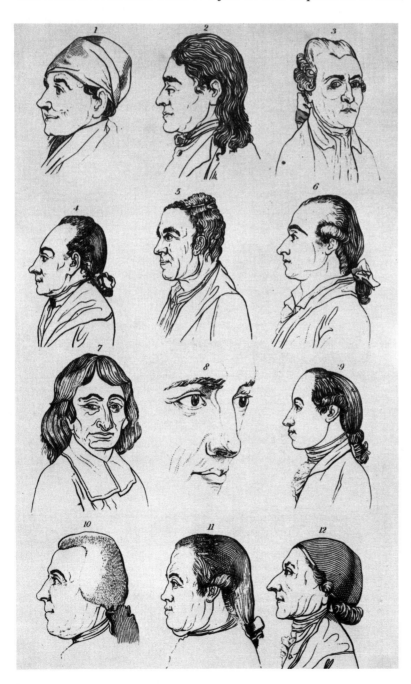

Although J. K. Lavater did not succeed in his goal of making physiognomy an exact science, he gained fame for his skill in reading character from a person's appearance, especially the face. His book *Physiognomical Fragments* was published in the 1770s, and would be called a best seller in today's terms. In his book, Lavater gave these examples of how to read faces.

1 No strength of mind, shown most clearly in the area around the eyes. Also shows commonness.

2 None of the features point to strength of mind, but none can be pinpointed as showing weakness.

3 A resolute, industrious, and enterprising person, ready and able to undertake big projects.

4 The eyes and nose in particular tell of sincerity, frankness, and sensibility. A benevolent person.

5 There is something of the eager inquirer left in this face, but it has distorted and become gross.

6 Quick perception, charm, and grace. The forehead, eyebrow, and poetical eyes are the sure signs.

7 A terrifying face because the qualities of power, daring, and eloquence are void of grace.

8 The eyes denote a thinker; the nose, an accurate investigator; the mouth, eloquence.

9 A face of noble character, including sincerity, fortitude, humor, perseverance, harmony.

10 Understanding and originality mark the face of a poet. There is also tranquility and taste.

11 Another person of poetic genius, but more vigorous than elegant. Strength, fidelity, and sweetness.

12 Lavater's face, on which he says: ". . . the commentary is before the world—in this book."

two faces perfectly alike, so it is impossible to find two people whose hands resemble each other perfectly."

His views were echoed by true scientists of the 19th century. These included the naturalist Charles Darwin, who wrote a study of the *Expression of the Emotions in Men and Animals*, and the Italian anthropologist Paolo Mantegazza, who concentrated on the difference between eyes, noses, and upper lips, and made them the basis of his "abbreviated portrait of all faces." He, and those who later carried on his work, divided the face into three sections: the forehead, the nose, and the area from the base of the nose to the point of the chin. In reading each of these divisions, he stated that the longer the forehead, the brainier the person; the longer the nose, the more energetic

Above: poking fun at the idea of reading character from the bumps on one's head, this 19th-century engraving shows a phrenologist painting bumps—presumably all the desirable ones—on a child's clean shaven head.

Left: the 20th century seems to have a machine for everything. This mechanical device of 1907 was meant for use by phrenologists.

65

This 19th-century cartoon also jokes about phrenology. As the lecturer whips off his wig to reveal the bumpiest head imaginable, the members of his audience register wonderment and awe.

and forceful the person; the longer the mouth and chin, the more determined and dogged the person. From there he moved to the eyes—"the windows of the soul"—saying that large eyes denote someone eager and observant, while small eyes denote someone calculating and shrewd; wide-set eyes indicate someone reliable and trusting, and close-set eyes belong to a man or woman who is suspicious, cynical, and on the defensive.

To some extent, Mantegazza's work inspired the Italian criminologist Cesare Lombroso, who believed that criminals fell into definite physical types. These types included those possessing handle-shaped ears, outsize jaws, and high cheekbones. Taking such features into account, Lombroso said that he could predict who would become a thief or a forger. Along with most palmists of the time, he believed that a potential killer could be spotted by his "murderer's thumb"—one with a bulbous nail-bearing joint. His work was much ridiculed, and Lombroso became embittered by failure.

Recently, American researchers have suggested a link between abnormal palm prints and congenital physical defects and disorders. They think it possible that the so-called "simian line"—in which the heart and head lines appear as one—and a broad Y-shape on the palm running from the wrist and branching

J. K. Lavater, 18th-century pioneer of physiognomy, laid down exact rules for reading character from the face. Here are three of his interpretations: The face above reveals a despicable nature. Greed, craftiness, and viciousness are fully shown in the mouth, eyes, and facial contours.

This face shows up a cheat or con man, even though the pointed nose and chin indicate a winning personality. The long and wide forehead points to a deep thinker; but taken in all, the face is of an untrustworthy man.

The man with this face is a heavy drinker, and this is seen in every one of its features. The nose, the lips, the wrinkles —all suggest an "unquenchable thirst." There is a lack of energy in the look, and the whole face has been altered. It is puffy, wrinkled, and very ruddy.

out toward the index and little fingers, can be signs of mongolism or some other mental retardation.

In his final years, Lombroso turned to spiritualism for solace. In some ways, his career and fate paralleled that of the German physician Franz Joseph Gall, who was the founder of the system of *phrenology*—reading of character by bumps on the head. According to Gall, he was a schoolboy when he first noticed that the most outstanding scholars were those with "prominent eyes and, even more significantly, certain peculiarities in the shapes of their heads, the shapes caused by variations in the development of certain areas on the surface of the brain." On graduating from university, he spent several years visiting schools, prisons, and lunatic asylums, where he studied, felt, and measured hundreds of skulls. Calling his system a "scientific form of divination," he used his calipers to discover whether or not a subject had an "underdeveloped organ of benevolence" or an "overgrown organ of theft."

On one notable occasion, Gall received a box of skulls from a prison doctor, and selected one with abnormally wide temples. "My God"! he exclaimed, "this is the cranium of a thief"! His diagnosis was correct, and he might have made a name for himself. However, his system was abused by scores of

## The Mysterious Meaning of Moles!

The study of moles for fortune telling takes into account the shape, color, and location of them on the body.

Round moles point to goodness of nature; angular ones stand for good and bad characteristics; oblong ones denote a degree of material well-being. Light moles are thought to indicate luck; black ones tell of difficulties to overcome before final success will be achieved.

Some of the meanings of moles by location are as follows:

*Belly* — a tendency to self-indulgence. Watch out for overeating, overdrinking, and overspending. Marry someone calm and understanding.

*Buttocks*—lack of ambition. The tendency is to accept whatever comes along, even if it's poverty.

*Chin* — a first-rate character and personality. A host of good qualities, such as generosity, lovingness, competence, responsibleness.

*Finger* — dishonesty. This comes mainly from an inclination to exaggerate because of inability to face reality.

quacks and charlatans who toured the salons and fairgrounds of central Europe. Gall himself was attacked and ridiculed by priests and fellow doctors. His lectures in Vienna were shouted down by his opponents, and, when he later settled in Paris, he again saw his new "science" mocked and ignored.

The English poet and mystic William Blake, who was of the same era as Gall, also believed that a person's face said what a person was. As a schoolboy of 13, Blake was taken by his father to see an engraver named Ryland. Leaving the engraver's premises, William turned to his father and said: "I don't like that man." "Why not?" asked his father. "His face," replied the boy, "looks as if he will yet be hanged." Twelve years later, in 1783, Ryland was hanged for forging banknotes, and for the rest of his life, Blake tended to judge people by their features and physical appearance. In this, he agreed with the essayist Joseph Addison that "a good face is a letter of introduction."

In the 19th century, the art of palmistry began to stage a comeback in Paris. Encouraged by the silence of royalty and the new and apparent broadmindedness of the clergy, a cluster of palmists appeared on the scene. They worked on the theory that each person "knows" his own future, whether he realizes it or not, and that the lines on his palms can help him get at this knowledge. So popular did they become that they had to turn clients away.

Prominent among this latest breed of fortune tellers was the stout and bespectacled Madame Adele Moreau, who announced that she would receive querants "every day except Sunday and Feast Days, between the hours of nine and six." For those who either couldn't gain entrance or come in person, she would "take consultations by post in the form of photographs and prints." Her autobiographical book about her career was a best seller, with its intimate and revealing accounts of the people—both famous and unknown—who came to her with problems that would have taxed a present-day psychiatrist.

Madame Moreau's male counterpart was the same Casimir D'Arpentigny who formulated the seven types of hands already described. He also designated two main classes of hands—the "smooth" and the "knotty." The hand with smooth fingers he found embodied "impressionability, caprice, spontaneity, and intuition, with a sort of momentary inspiration . . . and a faculty which gave the power of judging at first sight." It was invariably the sign of the artist. Compared with this, a hand with knotty fingers reflected "order, aptitude for number, and an appreciation of the exact sciences . . . mathematicians, agriculturists, architects, engineers, and navigators; all, in short, who were led to the application of acquired knowledge."

A hero of Napoleon's army before he retired at the age of 48, D'Arpentigny laid the foundations for those who were to bring palmistry into the 20th century, both in Great Britain and the USA. His findings and working methods were discussed throughout Europe, and it was written of them that: "As water falling drop by drop upon stones makes, in the course of time, a visible impression . . . so the mind, acting at every instant of time upon the plastic susceptibility of the hand, leaves ultimately signs which are accepted by the chiromancist

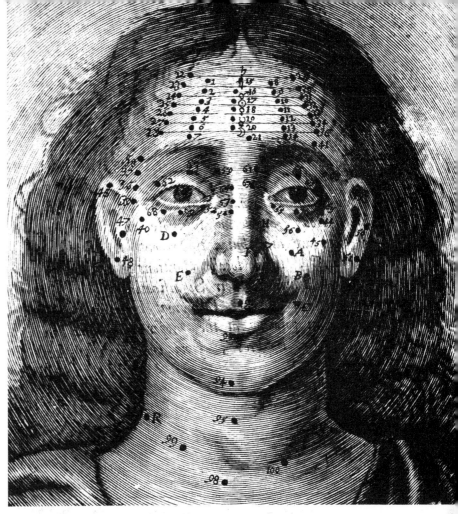

Right: a woman who laments about a mole on her face might be happier if she knew it could foretell good things—depending on its position. Instructions for telling fortunes from moles were usually included in the dream books of the late 19th century.

Below: one of the less well-known psychic practices is the interpretation of lines on the forehead. It dates from the 16th century.

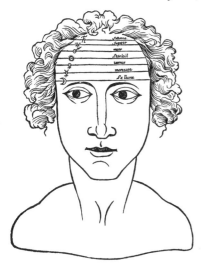

as the visible records of the impulses emanating from the great nervous center."

In April 1889, the English Chirological Society came into being in London with the express purposes of, "firstly, raising the study of the hand to the level of scientific research; secondly, for promoting the study of Palmistry in all its branches; thirdly, as a safeguard to the public against charlatans and impostors." This was the climate in which Cheiro first opened his consulting room in England—although he soon found that "the hands of men of God" were turned against him.

"I had not been in London one month," he wrote, "before a Catholic priest refused to give absolution to an entire family because they had consulted me against his orders. In America, during my first year, I was visited by two clergymen, with the object of persuading me that my success was due alone to the agency of the devil. One went so far as to tell me that God had sent him to offer me a clergyship—at a small salary, of course— if I would only give up my relations with the Evil One."

Apart from his supposed association with the devil, Cheiro gained more ecclesiastical enemies by contending that biblical scholars had mistranslated the seventh verse of the 37th chapter of Job. In the accepted English version, it read: "God sealed up the hands of men that all men may know God's work." The palmist insisted that, in the original Hebrew, it went: "God placed signs and marks in the hands of all the sons of men that all men might know their works." Cheiro's version was accepted by his thousands of clients and disciples, who felt as he did that the Church was "too obstinate" to admit that forecasting the future by palmistry was divinely inspired. Another aspect of Cheiro's system dealt with the time at which changes would occur in a person's life. He based his system on the ancient Greeks, who, in their study of the hand, considered that a person did not enter into the "battle of life" until he was 21. Cheiro placed the period of 25-to-35 years of age as the critical one in the "struggle for existence." "It is in reality the foundation on which man builds for the following 35 years," he stated. "If he has not by the middle of his life done something to warrant his existence, it is not to be expected that he would make much out of the remaining half."

In his first season in London, Cheiro was asked to read hands from behind curtains as a test of his skills. Unable to see the subject's face or general appearance, he was still able to make predictions that sometimes startled the client, and even shook society. Such was the case on the day he was invited to a large reception and asked to read "a somewhat soft and flabby" pair of hands without seeing or knowing who their owner was. "You are a famous man," said the palmist after studying the hands, "and are at the very height of your success now. However, your Lines of Fate and Success are broken just seven years further on. You must beware of taking any precipitate action then. If you do it will be the ruin of you." At this the client— the Irish playwright Oscar Wilde—pulled his hands away and

Above: Cheiro, whose real name was Count Louis Hamon, did much to make palmistry popular by his often reprinted books. Many of his clients were rich and famous. Below: Cheiro's consulting room was richly furnished, and had the atmosphere of the occult about it.

said gravely to the assembled guests: "Cheiro may be right. As fate keeps no road-menders on her highways—*Che Sara Sara*—what is to be, will be." Seven years and two trials later, Wilde was imprisoned for homosexuality after a notorious legal battle. "This otherwise clever man," said Cheiro of Wilde, "could not realize that the 'road-mender' was in himself. He made no change in his habits, and so he went headlong to his doom."

Throughout his long and prosperous career, Cheiro repeatedly said that actually seeing into the future was only one, and perhaps not even the most significant, aspect of divination. Most important was what a person did or did not do when coming events were revealed to him. For, said Cheiro, although the event itself may be predestined, its effects were not, and it was in the power of the individual to make its effects either beneficial or harmful. As Cheiro typically and dramatically put it in his book *You and Your Hand*:

"An engine driver may receive a warning in advance that a broken bridge some 10 or 20 miles ahead spells catastrophe for himself and the train he is driving. If he is a sensible man he will accept the warning—wait for the bridge to be repaired—and so save his life and the lives of others. If, on the contrary, he is too stupid or headstrong to be guided by the knowledge he has gained he will dash on to destruction . . . In all such cases the 'broken bridge' might have been repaired—but those terrible words 'too late' too often turn life into a tragedy instead of the beautiful creation it might have been."

Like many others in his field, Cheiro was intrigued by the study of murder, especially of deciding which person was likely in the "right circumstances" to kill, and which person was not. "The fact that one man kills another in a fit of uncontrollable passion or blind fury," he wrote in *You and Your Hand*, "is no more or less an accident that may occur to anyone who has not cultivated self-control. In such cases the Head Line is generally short and coarse-looking, with a brutal looking thumb . . . There is, however, another class of murderer—that of the brooding, melancholy type. In this class the Head Line is generally shown in a kind of jumble of Head and Heart Lines with a sloping line from this formation to, or toward, the Mount of Luna. In this case the man would brood for years over some real or fancied wrong, generally proceeding in some way from the affections. Examples may be read in the newspapers almost every day of men who murder their wives and sometimes their entire family. From the standpoint of study, the most interesting class of murderer is the poisoner. Here calculation, patience, caution, intelligence all play their role. In consequence, the Line of Head would naturally be expected to be long, finely marked, and connected with the Life Line to give it extreme caution."

The infamous Doctor Crippen, who poisoned his wife and dismembered her body in their North London home, was a clear example of the second kind of killer. Cheiro—who was also a numerologist—worked out a complicated chart which showed that the numbers 4 and 8 had proved fatal to Crippen. He was born in 1862, which adds up to 17, which in turn

Above: Oscar Wilde was the subject of a test for Cheiro, who, at a society party, was challenged to read the famous writer's hand from behind a curtain. If Wilde had listened to the palmist's warning of ruin from "precipitate action" in seven years' time, he might have saved himself from imprisonment and public scorn.

Above: this is the hand print of one of history's best-known women spies—Mata Hari. It shows where her life line was crossed and cut in her 37th year—when she died. Cheiro made this imprint of her hand 17 years before she was executed for spying by the French.

Left: Mata Hari wore a skimpy costume when she did what she called a Javanese dance. She performed at private parties where she met the rich and influential men of Paris. Her real name was Lady Cresta Macleod.

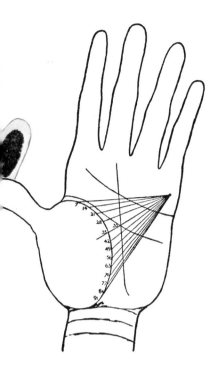

**Above: this chart was devised by Cheiro to show how to predict when in life certain events—such as illness or change—will occur.**

**Below: this is the hand print of Dr. Meyer, a notorious poisoner. Cheiro read it without knowing who it belonged to, and, because the life line was unbroken at that given point, predicted that its owner would not be put to death. Cheiro was right: Dr. Meyer was pardoned at the eleventh hour.**

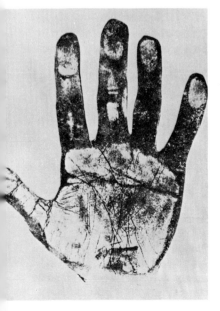

ultimately adds up to 8; he killed his wife on the 31st (4); her mutilated remains were discovered in his cellar on the 13th (4); and while trying to escape, he used the name Robinson (8 letters). He was recognized and arrested aboard the ship *Montrose* (8 letters) on the 22nd (4), and was brought back to England on the *Megantic* (8 letters). Crippen's formal arrest took place on the 31st (4), his trial ended on the 22nd (4), and he was hanged when he was 48 years old.

Cheiro was not personally involved in the Crippen case, so it took another murder case to bring the palmist to the notice of the public. This was the case of the killer physician, Dr. Meyer. Impressions of Meyer's hands were given to Cheiro during his first visit to New York, when reporters from the *New York World* sought to test his powers. Without knowing whose prints they were, or anything about Meyer, Cheiro stated: "Whether this man has committed one crime or 20 is not the question. As he enters his 44th year he will be tried for murder and condemned to death. It will then be found that for years he has used his intelligence and whatever profession he has followed to obtain money by crime, and has stopped at nothing to achieve his ends. He will be sentenced to death, yet his hands show his life will not end in this manner. He will live for years—but in prison."

Meyer, who was then 44, had at that very time less than a week to go before he was to be strapped into the electric chair in Sing-Sing prison. One of his last requests was to speak to the celebrated palmist, and Cheiro obligingly went up to the jail. There he met the "completely broken" man, who gasped: "For God's sake, tell me if you stand by your words that I shall escape the chair." Cheiro calmed the condemned man down, telling him that his Line of Life went on "clear and distinct" well past his 44th year, and that it showed no sign of a break. With that, Cheiro returned to his hotel.

"Day after day went past," he recorded in his last book *You and Your Hand*, "with no news to relieve the tension. The evening papers, full of details of the preparations for the execution fixed for the next morning, were eagerly bought up. I bought one and read every line. Midnight came. Suddenly boys rushed through the streets screaming 'special edition.' I read across the front page, 'Meyer escapes the chair. Supreme Court finds flaw in indictment.' The miracle had happened— the sentence was altered to imprisonment for life. Meyer lived on for 15 years. When the end did come, he died peacefully in the prison hospital."

As with all forms of fortune telling, palmistry is concerned with death—how, when, and where one will die. It is a question that is frequently asked, and infrequently answered. The majority of palmists know the danger of revealing such information to a client, especially if the person is nervous or emotional. Subconsciously, such a querant may bring about his or her own doom by behaving in a rash or suicidal way. "In such instances," said Cheiro, "it is better to remain silent, and to risk being called a fool or a fraud. The most important quality a responsible palmist can have is humility, the humility to know when it is kinder and more Christian not to speak."

# 5

# Revealing the Tarot's Secrets

Two hours before attempting to beat his own world record, British motorboat racer Donald Campbell decided to tell his fortune by the cards. He shuffled a pack and drew two cards that made him grow pale and shake his head—the Ace and the Queen of Spades. "These are the same cards that Mary Queen of Scots turned over on the

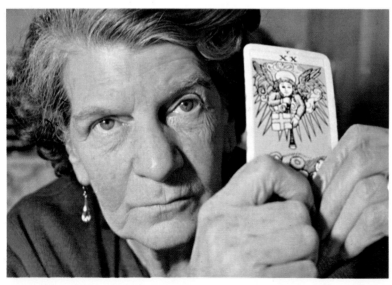

Right: in this modern version of the Tarot death card, a skeleton does a whirlwind dance while brandishing a scythe. It was designed by Aleister Crowley, one of the most colorful occult figures of the 20th century. Crowley believed that the Tarot dated from ancient Egypt, a theory he explained and defended in his last work, *The Book of Thoth*.

Left: Madame Nicole reads Tarot cards in a lean-to shed behind one of the busiest streets of London—and earns a good living. She's been doing this work since she was 17, and says: "It's noble work, if you do it religiously."

TRUMPS  Death  m

# "If he'd heeded the cards he would be alive now"

night before her execution," he told watching friends. "I think that someone in my family will die soon." This scene took place on the morning of January 4, 1967. Those present were horrified when, a short time later, Campbell's jet speedboat *Bluebird* reared up on her tail while skimming over Coniston Water in the English Lake District, and turned a back somersault at almost 300 miles per hour. The boat plunged 140 feet to the bottom of the lake, and, although Royal Navy divers later brought up sections of the hull, Campbell's body was not recovered. "If he'd heeded the cards," one of his friends said later, "he would be alive now." A superstitious person for most of his life, Campbell read cards much as others read the daily newspaper. He believed that the future could be seen in them. What he probably didn't realize was that the ordinary pack of 52 playing cards he used was based on the 78 cards of the Tarot, a set of mystical cards hundreds—perhaps thousands—of years old.

Although the origin of the Tarot has never been fully explained, the colorful cards have a long history. One of the earliest proven dates of their appearance is 1329, when there is a record of them in Germany. However, some occultists believe that the Tarot dates back to Egyptian civilization, and

Above: the speedboat *Bluebird* reared into the air at the start of the accident that took the life of Donald Campbell, then the world water speed record holder. It happened on Coniston Water in the Lake District of England. Above right: the racing boat then turned a complete back somersault. Far right: from the somersault, *Bluebird* plunged into the water and sank. It went 140 feet down. Right: Donald Campbell, dressed in his usual way for boat racing. A believer in signs, Campbell had told his fortune from the cards just before his final race—and had drawn two cards of bad omen.

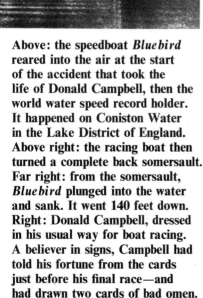

76

others find evidence for their existence between these two periods. With no one able to disprove their claims, such different groups as gypsies and the crusading Knights Templar asserted that the Tarot was their creation. Whichever of the many theories is accepted, it is indisputable that the cards have long endured—both as a fortune-telling method and as a game.

The word itself derives from the use of the cards for play. In 14th-century Italy, they were the basis of a game called *tarocco*. When France adopted the game, they also adapted the name, which became *tarot* in French. Even though it is the French name that has stuck, it is more likely the Italian deck from which the present-day deck of playing cards has been developed.

The traditional Tarot deck has 78 cards, and the symbolic pictures on them are much the same as they have been through the ages. There are 22 picture cards called Major or Greater Arcana, Trumps, Triumphs, or Atouts. Generally speaking, they represent the spiritual and cosmic forces affecting mankind, such as power, faith, death, and courage. Each of these symbolic picture cards has a title, most of which express mightiness. Among them are Jupiter, The World, Justice, The Empress and The Emperor, Death, Star, Moon, and Sun. They

Above: these are the two unlucky cards that Campbell picked from the pack on the day he died in a speedboat accident—the Queen and Ace of Spades. Campbell said they were the same cards drawn by Mary Queen of Scots on the night before her execution.

The Tarot suit known as Batons, Scepters, or Wands is Clubs today.

From the Tarot's Cups or Coupes has come the modern suit of Hearts.

**Above:** modern playing cards developed out of the 56-card Minor Arcana of the Tarot, which has four suits containing nonsymbolic picture cards and plain cards. The number of cards was reduced to 52 by the combination of the knight and the page into a jack. **Below:** it doesn't have to be a Tarot deck for fortune telling by cards. This French engraving shows playing cards being used.

are also numbered, except for The Fool. This card has no number, but is nonetheless essential to the deck.

Another 56 cards, called the Minor Arcana, are divided into four suits. Picture cards also appear among these, but they are familiar rather than symbolic—King, Queen, Knight, and Page. The Tarot suits are swords or epees; batons, scepters, or wands; cups or coupes; and coins, deniers, or pentacles. These cards broadly represent occupations or careers and social position.

Another distinctive feature of the Tarot cards is that they are not the same when turned from top to bottom, and can

The Swords or Epees of the Tarot has developed into the present Spades.

What was Coins, Pentacles, or Deniers in the Tarot is now Diamonds.

best be read in the upright position. If they appear inverted during a reading, their meaning is altered—or even reversed.

The playing cards used today came from the 56 cards of the Minor Arcana, plus The Fool. Because the Knight and the Page were combined into the Jack, the modern deck has only 52 cards. The Fool has become the Joker, but it is very much an extra, being important in only a few games. As for the suits, spades has its source in swords, clubs in batons, hearts in cups, and diamonds in coins.

The Tarot as a means of telling fortunes is said to contain an entire symbolic system that provides a "key to the mysteries,"

**Below: a street fortune teller in present-day Marrakesh, Morocco, uses the traditional Tarot cards.**

## LA PAPESSA

The second card of the Major Arcana went through a change from a Lady Pope to a High Priestess.

**Above:** in the early Italian Tarot packs of the 14th century, the card showed a female pope in both name and garb—probably based on the legendary Pope Joan of five centuries previous.

**Right:** in more modern Tarot decks, this card is illustrated by a priestess in both name and dress. The 1910 design of the High Priestess by occultist A. E. Waite has robes that hint strongly of origins in ancient Egypt.

and "holds the secret of the true nature of man, the universe, and God." Those versed in the use of the Tarot believed that there was nothing about man and his destiny that could not be revealed by these cards. The acceptance by many people of the Tarot's powers meant that it would eventually come into conflict with the Church. It did so, and in 1377, a Swiss monk came out with the first recorded diatribe against the Tarot in particular, and playing cards in general.

However, the production and use of playing cards grew. Only two years after the Swiss monk's public condemnation of cards, the ledgers of the Belgian Duke of Brabant contained the first recorded purchase of cards in his country. Later that

## THE HIGH PRIESTESS

same year of 1379, playing cards was described as a pastime at a fete in Brussels.

The Tarot appeared in splendid forms at royal courts, in noble castles, and in rich manor houses. In 1392, King Charles VI of France commissioned the painting of three packs of cards that became famous as near works of art. They were done by the artist Gringonneur. He painted them on gold-edged, silver-backed vellum, using lapis lazuli for the beautiful sky blue color, and a rich red pigment known as "mummy's dust." Seventeen of these unique cards still survive, and are preserved in the Bibliothèque Nationale in Paris.

The Gringonneur cards deviated from the original spirit of the Tarot in that the pictures were more on the pretty side than powerful and brooding. In the following century, similar cards were painted for the Duke of Milan and other powerful families of Northern Italy. Despite their cost and the artistic effort that had gone into them, the Tarot cards were again condemned—this time by St. Bernadin of Siena in 1423. His attack resulted in the burning of numerous packs, among them some choice ones.

After this, both political and religious rulers of Europe made efforts to stifle the growth of the Tarot cards. The pious considered them as a "pagan challenge" to the Church, and forbade their use on grounds of their being unholy. It was on economic grounds, however, that the Venetian authorities in 1441 and the English king in 1463 banned their importation. In time, these prohibitions worked against the popularity of the Tarot, and people sought other, easier ways of trying to see into their futures. To consult the Tarot became a harmless game or pastime, like playing ordinary cards. It wasn't until near the end of the 18th century that the Tarot was again taken seriously as a means of reaching out into the future.

The man responsible for this revival was the learned French writer Antoine Court de Gebelin, whose lifework was the preparation and publication of a mammoth book *The Old World Analyzed and Compared With the New World*. Nine volumes of the uncompleted work appeared between 1773 and 1784. Volume eight, which came out in Paris in 1781, contained a section called "The Fame of Tarot." In that section, Gebelin wrote: "If one were to know that in our days there existed a work of ancient Egypt, one of their books that escaped malicious destruction . . . a book about their most pure and interesting doctrines, everybody would be eager no doubt to know such an extraordinary and precious work."

Gebelin himself had been introduced to the Tarot at a friend's house, and with his usual display of wide knowledge, declared that the cards had "doubtless originated in Egypt." He felt confirmed in this point of view after further research, when he stated that the Tarot was no less than the remains of the famous Egyptian book of magical learning, the Book of Thoth. "There is no doubt whatsoever in my mind," he stated, "that the Tarot images and symbols contain the answers to the occult powers and wisdom of the ancient world. And what had validity and was in force then is also present in our modern times."

His imaginative view of the Tarot's origins was largely dis-

The stories about Pope Joan—now believed highly unfounded—were picked up by English Protestants in the 17th century for anti-Catholic propaganda. This frontispiece of a book published in London in 1675 shows the discovery of Pope Joan as a woman when she has a baby during a holy procession. Some Tarot authorities believe that Pope Joan was the source for the Lady Pope card.

This artistic representation of The Sun was part of the Tarot deck painted by Gringonneur for King Charles VI of France in the 14th century. The few cards that remain from this deck show it to have been a near work of art.

proved after the discovery of the Rosetta Stone in 1799, which led to the deciphering of early Egyptian writing. Meantime, however, his ideas were ardently taken up by a Parisian wig maker and barber named Alliette, who proceeded to restore what he said were the original Egyptian designs to the cards. Declaring that both the pictures and their meanings had been distorted over the centuries, Alliette brought out a series of extremely popular books about the Tarot. "I have studied the mysteries of the cards for more than 30 years," he said, "and it is only now that I am beginning to understand them at their truest and deepest level."

Despite the intellectual exertion required to learn and read the mysteries of the Tarot, it found thousands of new followers during the time of Napoleon. The emperor was well known as a firm believer in fortune telling. He even had his own personal and highly complicated Book of Fortune, which he consulted before each of his battles. The Little Emperor was impressed by the talents of Marie Lenormand, who used a set of Tarot cards of her own design, and by which she predicted his marriage to Josephine. Later, she was appointed as an attendant to the Empress. Even so, Napoleon twice imprisoned her for making prophecies not in accordance with his plans, and became violently angry when she told him that the cards foretold of his death by either rope or bullet. (His disposition was not improved when the seeress also lost her temper and threw her Tarot pack in his face.)

For the next few decades of the early 19th century, Tarot readers continued to turn up The Hanging Man, The Juggler, The Fool, The Devil, and all the other traditional card symbols throughout the fashionable salons of France. Their influence was not as strongly felt in any other European country, however. For example, there had been no recorded use of the Tarot in England since the late 16th century, when Henry Cuffe, secretary to the Earl of Essex, had consulted someone to read the cards for him. That card reader told Cuffe to draw three cards from a Tarot pack, and to place them face downward on a table. Cuffe did so, and then, as instructed, turned over the cards in the same order he had drawn them. The first was a full-length picture of a man under the escort of armed soldiers; the second showed a grim-faced judge; the third a gallows. At the time Cuffe laughed at the clear omens—especially that of the hangman. However, on March 13, 1601, he was found guilty of treason against Queen Elizabeth I. He was then taken to the Tyburn, the public hanging place of London, and "hanged by the neck until he was dead."

Interest in the Tarot held fast in France during the 19th century. One of its leading practitioners was Alphonse Louis Constant, who used the pen name of Eliphas Lévi. Lévi brought a deeper meaning to the use and interpretation of the Tarot. After being educated at a Catholic seminary and being ordained as a deacon, he left the church to marry a girl of 16. When she deserted him—taking their two children with her— Lévi turned to the study of the occult for consolation. He showed a particular interest in the Tarot, which he regarded as being linked with the Cabala. This occult system of thought

Above: the traditional in Tarot design is represented by this card from the Swiss IJJ deck, said to be some centuries old.
Center: another traditional design from the Marseilles pack.
Right: A. E. Waite's design of 1910 was more romanticized.

Left: Egyptian themes dominate Aleister Crowley's Tarot design.
Above: this new Tarot card of the Magician was especially commissioned for a James Bond movie.

originated with Jewish mystics of the 2nd or 3rd century, and is one of the oldest schools of mystical belief in the world. For many centuries, the Cabala was regarded as the true key to all the mysteries of the universe. It influenced almost every philosopher from the period of its founding to the late 13th century. It had many advocates in later eras, and still has today.

In 1856, Lévi published a book entitled *The Ritual of High Magic*. In it he states: "The universal key of magical works is that of all ancient religious dogmas—the key of the Cabala and the Bible. . . . Now, this Clavicle [The Tarot], regarded as lost for centuries, has been recovered by us, and we have been able to open the sepulchres of the ancient world, to make the dead speak, to behold the monuments of the past in all their splendor, to understand the enigmas of every sphinx, and to penetrate all sanctuaries. Among the ancients the use of this key was permitted to none but the high priests, and even so its secret was confided only to the flower of initiates."

Even though he considered himself a "flower of initiates," Lévi never had the time or patience to design a complete set of Tarot cards in line with his ideas. Such a set would have had to include "the Sacred Tree," a cabalistic diagram of the "anatomy of God." It consists of ten circles joined by 22 lines— the circles being spiritual states, and the lines paths to them. The design on which most modern European packs are based was bequeathed by a follower of Lévi's named Oswald Wirth, and his ideas were later spread by Dr. Gerard Encausse. Like Lévi, Encausse believed that the Tarot had come to Europe by way of the gypsies.

Encausse followed the example of the majority of Tarot experts of the 18th and 19th centuries by writing under a pseudonym. This was probably done both as a bit of showmanship and as a way to protect themselves and their relatives from possible ridicule and abuse. Encausse used the name Papus in his writings on the Tarot, which he described as the "Bible of Bibles." He and Lévi were largely responsible for the popularization of the Tarot in the central countries of Europe. As far as the United States and Britain were concerned, the cards were in other prophets' hands.

In 1887, London saw the founding of the Hermetic Order of the Golden Dawn. This group followed Lévi's teachings in some respects, but differed greatly from them in others. The Golden Dawn was put on the occult map mainly through the efforts of a man who called himself MacGregor Mathers, or Le Compte de Glenstrae. Its system was also based on that of the Cabala, and held that the Sacred Tree could be climbed by man until he comes into some form of contact with God. The 22 cards of the Major Arcana were linked both with the 22 paths of the Sacred Tree and the 22 letters of the Hebrew alphabet. In this cabalistic formulation of the cards, the attempt was made to show the relation between God, Man, and the Universe. Mathers and other members of the Golden Dawn also made changes in the design of, and gave different meanings to, the Tarot.

The various designs and conflicting interpretations can make things difficult for the student of the Tarot, especially if he or

**Above: Napoleon and his wife Josephine are constantly described as deep believers in all kinds of fortune telling. Mlle. Lenormand, here shown reading cards for the Empress, was said to have a great influence with the couple.**

**Above: Napoleon is shown with an Egyptian soothsayer who, according to many reports, predicted his divorce and his later exile.**
**Below left: in this engraving, Napoleon consults an Italian astronomer.**

she is a beginner. However, by dispensing with the Minor Arcana and making a formal, straightforward spread of the Major, it is possible for the amateur to give a not unsatisfactory reading of the cards. This stems from the activation of the subconscious, which, according to Tarot expert Richard Gardner, frequently brings about quick results. "The merest amateur, who has still to look up lists of card meanings while reading a spread, will often give a little message that is quite valid or useful," he stated.

Before the cards are laid out, however, there are other conditions that must be observed, and other factors that the would-be diviner must bring into focus. In his comprehensive book, *The Occult*, Colin Wilson suggests that, for utmost impact, the student should be imbued with a feeling for the Middle Ages. "The mind," he writes, "should be full of images of Gothic cathedrals, of medieval stained glass . . . of small towns surrounded by fields, and artisans at their everyday work. Without this kind of preparation, the skeptical modern mind is likely to attach its own associations to cards like The Pope, The High Priestess . . . and The Devil." Whether or not this

# The Major Arcana of the Tarot

There are altogether 78 cards in the Tarot deck, but the most important of them, with the richest significance, are the 22 cards of the Major Arcana. Traditionally, in reading the Tarot cards, the Major Arcana represents the physical and spiritual forces that act upon mankind. Unlike the ordinary double-headed playing cards, Tarot cards have a single picture which alters in meaning if inverted. Here the interpretations are given for both upright (▲) and inverted (▼) cards.

### The Fool

LE MAT.

The unnumbered card.

▲ Immaturity, lack of consideration, thoughtlessness. One drawing this card should take care to exercise will power in order to overcome foolishness, and to make the correct choices in life.
▼ To make the wrong choice; to stop or hesitate in life's progress. Apathy or negligence.

### The Emperor

L'EMPEREUR

▲ The card that symbolizes worldly power, competence, skill, and the domination of intelligence and reason over emotion and the passions. Realization of goals.
▼ Immaturity; lack of strength; weak character. Feebleness in action, a failure to control emotions, to get to grips with things.

### Jupiter or The Pope

JUPITER.

▲ Here is the symbol of mercy; a religious or spiritual person. Humility; kindness; leniency; or compassion. A person to whom other people go for help. Servitude; ritual; conformity; or forgiveness.
▼ Overkindness; the foolish exercise of generosity; frailty; also unorthodoxy, unconventionality.

### The Lovers

L'AMOUREUX.

▲ Not only the symbol of love, but of reconciliation. The necessity for testing, putting to the proof. Possible predicaments. Compatibility; harmony; beginning of a possible romance.
▼ Failure when put to the test. Unwise plans; infidelity; fickleness. The possibility of a wrong choice.

### The Wheel of Fortune

LA ROUE DE FORTUNE

▲ Symbol of the unending cycle of a changing universe. Advancement for better or possibly worse. Good fortune; luck; unexpected events. The full circle points to the course of events from start to finish.
▼ Bad luck. Sudden ill fate; a broken sequence; a break or inconsistency in what is expected.

### Strength

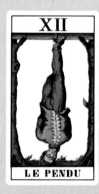

LA FORCE

▲ Courage; fortitude; energy; the needed strength to endure in spite of obstacles. Triumph of love over hate; hidden forces at work. Self-reliance; heroism. Strength and power, both physically and spiritually.
▼ Weakness; discord; the abuse of power; lack of faith. Overbearingness leading to tyranny.

### The Hanged Man

LE PENDU

▲ A life suspended; a point of transition; the changing of life's forces. Sacrifice; readjustment; rebirth. Effort and sacrifice may be called for to move toward a goal that may nonetheless not be reached.
▼ A lack of sacrifice; failure to give of one's self. Self-preoccupation.

### The House of God or The Lightning Struck Tower

LA MAISON DE DIEU

▲ A card that can mean catastrophe, but that also points to a better future. Breaking down of existing forms to make way for the new. Havoc. Breakdown. Terrible danger. Bankruptcy; loss of security. Loss of stability.
▼ Inability to make a necessary change. Continued oppression. Trapped; imprisoned.

### The Star

L'ÉTOILE

▲ A card symbolizing hope, faith, trust. A good omen; promise of opportunity; a bright future; optimism; favorable prospects. Insight; satisfaction; spiritual love.
▼ Hope unfulfilled. Bad luck; pessimism; a lack of opportunity; stubbornness. Possible harmony, but only short-lived.

### The Moon

LA LUNE

▲ The crayfish that creeps toward the girl symbolizes something that comes out of the unknown depths. Deception; trickery; insincerity; dishonesty. False friends; unknown enemies. Disillusionment.
▼ Minor deceptions, trifling mistakes. An uneasy peace after paying the necessary price.

### The Magician or The Juggler

▲The magician symbolizes originality and imagination, the ability to set one's own course, and the determination to see a chosen task all the way to completion. Mastery; self-control; skill; or subtlety. ▼Weakness of will or insecurity. Limited interest; delay; lack of imagination. Using skills for evil ends.

### Juno or The High Priestess

▲This card represents wisdom united with common sense; knowledge; intuition; understanding; education. She is a symbol of a good balance of intelligence and foresight. ▼Ignorance; shallowness; conceit; selfishness. One drawing it is apt to be satisfied with superficial knowledge.

### The Empress

▲The symbol of feminine productivity and action. Feminine progress; evolution; material wealth; fertility; marriage; the love of the good things in life. ▼Vacillation and indecision. A lack of concentration, leading to inaction and delay in getting things done. Anxiety.

### The Chariot

▲Trouble and adversity (which may possibly have been overcome already). Ordeal; obstacle; a great effort against overwhelming odds. Victory; triumph; greatness. ▼Defeat. Failure at the last moment to succeed; the sudden collapse of plans. Overwhelmed; a failure to meet and face responsibility.

### Justice

▲The pillar of moral strength and integrity, meaning justice; fairness; reasonableness; moderation; virtue; virginity; self-satisfaction in accomplishments. ▼Bias; intolerance; false accusations; abuse; bigotry; severity in judgment; unfairness.

### The Hermit

▲A card which represents wisdom and prudence; self-denial; thriftiness; withdrawal; silent counsel. It can indicate regression; desertion; or annulment. ▼Lack of patience, or possibly overprudence that can cause unnecessary delay. Immaturity; childishness; imprudence; foolishness.

### Death

▲The unlucky number 13 points to change and renewal rather than death itself. Clearing the way for transformation. Death of the old self, though not necessarily physical death. Ruin, end. ▼Stagnation; inertia; immobility. Change, but only a partial and incomplete one.

### Temperance

▲Moderation; temperance; self-control. Friendship; mixing or bringing together into a successful union. Reflection; harmony; compatibility; consolidation, fusion, patience; frugality. ▼Discord. Sterility; stubbornness; lack of patience; inability to work with others. Desires unfulfilled.

### The Devil

▲Bondage; subordination; black magic. A card of suffering, ravage, violence, shock, fatality—sometimes self-punishment. ▼Release from bondage; the realization that the ties can be broken. The first steps toward enlightenment; the beginning of spiritual understanding, of overcoming fear.

### The Sun

▲A card of triumph and achievement. Satisfaction; success; rewards through work. Engagement or a happy marriage. Moderation in life. Success in work; delight in daily life. ▼Triumph delayed, but perhaps not lost forever. Canceled plans; a broken engagement.

### Judgment

▲The rising figures suggest revival and reawakening. Rejuvenation; rehabilitation. A change of position. Readjustment; improvement; development; promotion. ▼Delay; failure to face facts. Separation, divorce. Indecision; procrastination; failure to find happiness.

### The World

▲The summing up of what all the other cards have said. Attainment; ultimate change; completion; success. The admiration of others. Triumph. ▼Imperfection; lack of vision. Failure to finish what has been started. Refusal to recognize the meanings given by the other cards.

All Tarot readings are highly personal, and it is difficult to lay down precise interpretations of each card. Until practice has sharpened a reader's intuition, an amateur card reader is probably well advised to start with the simplest of the Tarot spreads, which is the three-card spread. Here is a sample of what might come up in such a card reading.

## The Three Card Spread

Below: the King of Cups was chosen to represent a man who was fair-haired and 35 or over.

## Significator

ROI DE COUPE

medieval state of mind can be achieved, it is essential for the diviner to empty his head of everyday thoughts, and to concentrate on the mystic symbols. Once the meaning of the various cards has been learned—or jotted on the backs of the cards if necessary at the start—the reader will be ready to receive his first questioner. It is considered too introspective, and, therefore, too dangerous to tell your own fortune by means of the Tarot, because the magic of the cards can easily work against you.

By the time you give your first reading, your Tarot pack should have become personal to you, much as a pet becomes a kind of extension of its master. Two-way vibrations pass between the pack and its owner, and to protect this sensitive feeling, it is necessary to keep the cards away from anyone else. As a reader, you must become as familiar with your pack as possible, never using a new one for a reading. You should handle and study your Tarot pack as often as possible, so that a bridge is constructed between your subconscious and the Tarot symbols.

When not in use, the cards should be wrapped in a square of black or purple silk, and kept in a closed wooden box. As with the *I Ching* (see Chapter 3), the cards must be accorded a place of honor in the room. They should be kept on the side facing east—the direction from which the "light of inspiration" appears. The very fact that an object is regarded as having special powers can help the person believing in them to approach these powers himself. To increase your state of sensitivity, it helps if the room in which the reading is to be given is filled with incense. After a short period of meditation—perhaps ten minutes for beginners—some readers say in prayer, "God speaks through me." They ask their querant to observe a similar solemnity, for nothing can doom a Tarot reading more than a questioner who is merely out for a quick laugh.

You settle in a comfortable chair, and the querant sits across a table, on the south side facing north. Your seat opposite him is in keeping with the concealed currents of the earth, which are said to flow from north to south, from south to north. If you notice that the querant seems too stiff and awkward to allow a satisfactory reading, try to loosen him up with a cup of coffee or tea. If he seems too relaxed, try to impress on him the need to be alert and concentrated.

Providing the question has been serious and meaningful, the answer should be constructive. Again much depends upon you as the reader—how you interpret the inverted cards; whether you disbelieve the value of any sequential relationship; what value and significance you place on pairings. (For example, The Empress and The Emperor together can suggest either harmony or opposition.)

In doing your reading, you would be advised not to try forcing the cards, for they will fall as they will. By cooperating with the cards fully, you will sometimes find that the seeker's question was not the one he really wanted to ask, but a cover for some deeper underlying problem that was his true reason for consulting the Tarot. Having exposed this mental block,

Below: the querant sought an answer to the question, "Will I be able to provide for my family financially in the future?"
In reaching an answer, the first card showed that the querant had experienced past financial difficulties of a serious nature.
The second card said that those problems seemed to have been resolved, and the querant was at present financially stable.
The third card indicated that further setbacks will come, but that these will be surmounted if the querant exercises caution.

## Past

## Present

## Future

you can then coax him to talk about his basic worry—rather as a skillful doctor will ease the truth out of a patient who tries to minimize his symptoms. It is then that you can fully use the psychic energy at your disposal, and interpret the messages contained in the pack. "The cards," writes author Fred Gettings, "bear some resemblance to a highly refined Rorschach test in which the formless ink blots have been replaced by archetypal images which help the hidden truth in the spirit to reveal itself."

Now you start the reading. You take the 22 cards of the Major Arcana from their cover, spread the silk square over the flat surface of the table, and then carefully shuffle the pack so that there is an adequate mixture of upright and inverted designs. Remember that the cards must not be laid on anything

**3 Specific Goal**

**1 Present Influence**

LA LUNE

**4 Past Foundation**

LA JUSTICE

**2 Immediate Obstacles**

LE PENDU

**6 Future Influence**

L'AMOUREUX.

**5 Past Events**

## The Celtic Cross

This is the Celtic Cross spread, said to be easy and interesting. The querant is a young woman who asked, "Will I succeed in my career?" Her significator, the Knight of Cups for a light-haired person between 18 and 30, is hidden under card number 1.

1 The querant obviously wants to know if her accomplishments will be recognized.

2 The threat to her ambition is a tendency to be indiscreet and somewhat unmindful of others.

3 In the past, her abilities have been put to the test, and she has been proved worthy.

4 This card says the querant has been underhanded in her effort to get ahead.

5 There is a possibility of disappointment in her ambition.

6 In the near future, she will have a period of stagnation, and even sacrifice will go unnoticed.

7 She herself fears that impulsiveness will impede progress.

8 Friends are worried that the querant will sustain losses.

90

**9** There is hope of success in her work if she shows more appreciation of her co-workers.

**10** The egoism indicated by previous cards will be difficult to overcome, but her hopes can only be realized if she does.

**10 Final Result**

**9 Inner Emotions**

**8 Environmental Factors**

**7 The Questioner**

but the silk. The querant is requested to give a final shuffle, and you deal the spread you have chosen for the reading.

The first and most important card to be decided in a Tarot reading is the Significator, which is used to represent the questioner. This can be taken from the Minor Arcana. The choice is arbitrary, but should be made in keeping with the querant's personality or appearance. For example, the cups represent people with light brown hair or an indolent nature; the swords are for dark brown hair or tempestuousness; the wands for blonds or the active; the coins for the dark or the lazy. As far as age is concerned, the King or Queen fits someone who is over 35; the Knight, anyone between 18 and 30; and the Page, those under 18. The Significator is generally put face up in a central position on the table, and the spread is laid out face down beside it. Most beginning readers find that their strength and inspiration starts to drain after about a half hour, so they should choose one of the simplest spreads at first.

The least complicated of all the Tarot spreads is the three-card spread. This was the one used by the reader who predicted Henry Cuffe's fate. Of the three cards laid down in a row, the center one represents the querant in the present, the left one stands for the past, and the right one shows what might happen in the future. (Directions referred to are from the reader's point of view.)

Although it looks much more complicated, the Celtic cross spread is considered to be one of the easiest to master. It has the additional advantage of being interesting and rewarding. In this spread, 10 cards are used in total. Six of them are laid out in the form of a cross, and four go to the right in a straight up-and-down line. Instead of being face up, the Significator is covered by the first card. After the cards have been read in a sequence to show past and future influences, the answer to the specific question asked by the querant is revealed in the last card turned up.

Another spread that a beginner could try with fairly certain success is the seven-card spread. This is said to be particularly good for answering a "yes" or "no" question. All seven cards are laid out in a straight left-to-right line. Two cards stand for the past, three for the present, and two for the future—and the last card turned over gives the answer to the question asked.

The Tarot session is not over until the reader has completely dismissed the images from his conscious mind. Then, in accordance with tradition and occult protocol, he will go through the opening stages in reverse until the cards are safely back in their closed box pointing toward the sunrise. The beginning diviner and the querant may find themselves suffering from shyness or embarrassment. There is no valid reason why this should be so, but it might help if they think of eminent people in all professions and fields of endeavor who have found that the Tarot satisfied their desire to get an advance hint of the future—whether or not the hint was a favorable one.

Novelist Dennis Wheatley is a case in point. More than 40 years ago, he bought a Tarot pack and asked his wife—a gifted fortune teller with ordinary cards—to give a reading for him. The spread she laid was involved and complicated, and she puzzled long over it. Finally, Wheatley himself twice cut the pack, strictly against the Tarot code. Twice the Tower Struck by Lightning turned up, as though to tell him he would have to pay for his disregard of tradition.

"At worst," he related in his book *The Devil and All His Works*, "this card means violent death; at best when it is upside down, as was the case with both my cuts, it means heavy financial loss and possible imprisonment. I should have been greatly worried but, having no reason to anticipate such misfortune, laughed the matter off. However, a year later I had ample cause to recall this sinister indication of misfortune. For then, not only was I accused of fraud and faced with the threat of criminal proceedings; I might well have been sent to jail if an accountant had not, almost at the last minute, unearthed a document that exonerated me completely.

"It is by no means unusual for the Powers-that-Be to decree that we must suffer ill-fortune in order that our way of life be ultimately changed for the better. During the agonizing months that I could not go to my own office, and was debarred from taking a job with any other firm, I resolved to do my utmost to divert my mind from worry, so wrote an adventure story, *The Forbidden Territory*, and *A Private Life of King Charles II*. Both were published in 1933. They are both still widely bought and read."

Judging from Wheatley's experience, it can be seen that the effects of the Tarot predictions can be short-term. This is welcome news for those beginning their association with the so-called "Devil's cards." The relationship between the reader and his pack is like that of a modern computer and its operator — a balance of input and feedback, the one dependent upon and

## The Seven Card Spread

**Above:** the seven-card spread is supposed to be particularly good for a "yes" or "no" answer. The question in this case was, "Will I marry and be happy?"

**Opposite:** the significator is the Knight of Swords, to stand for a dark-haired young female.
1 Past relationships failed because of her lack of tolerance.
2 She has become more easy going, so recent relationships have been more satisfactory.
3 New understanding enables her to enjoy platonic friendships.

# Past          Present

**1 Distant Past**

**2 Immediate Past**

**3 Present Influences**  **4 Prese**

92

**CHEVALIER DES ÉPÉES**

**4** If she keeps her present outlook, it appears that she will make a happy marriage.
**5** She must resist the temptation to be emotional, and also avoid purely physical affairs.
**6** She will have to work to keep her marriage interesting.
**7** The final answer is "yes," but with a caution to heed the previous cards.

stimulated by the other. The Tarot is to be respected, but not feared, listened to, but not panicked by. On the highest level, and in the words of author Eden Gray, the skillful Tarot reader must:

"Go deep within in meditation; find your own divine center, and you will understand by direct intuition that which the Tarot only hints at—that which the mystics and philosophers who first designed the cards have been trying to convey to you in these picture-symbols."

In a more lighthearted vein—but not frivolously—America's "leading self-confessed witch" Sybil Leek sees the day when a Tarot pack will be as much a part of an average home as a dictionary, a refrigerator, or a vacuum cleaner. For the woman who wants to throw the party that has everything, a half-hour session with the Tarot will be obligatory.

"The fears of being thought 'odd' no longer apply to the hostess with a Tarot pack among her canapés," she asserts in *The Sybil Leek Book of Fortune-Telling*. "When prophecy takes place in the familiar, comfortable surroundings of a house, fear of being laughed at is dispelled . . . Perhaps only when we see the serious aspects of life as a game can we feel free to enjoy it . . . This may be the case with the Tarot cards. Once they were treated seriously throughout the world, then neglected and forgotten except by a chosen few in each generation who kept the art alive.

"Now they are finding favor as a parlor game. Those who know the occult significance of the Tarot cards can only hope that understanding is the next step in their exciting history." For the long-lived Tarot, this would merely mean a return to its former glory.

## Future

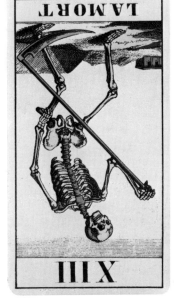

**Obstacles  5  Present Outlook        6  Future Influences      7  Ultimate Results**

# 6

# Pictures From the Future

Right: this newspaper illustration of 1879 points up the late 19th-century English belief that murderers are haunted by their dreams. It shows the dream of a well-known thief and murderer the night before his execution. In it, he sees his shiftless life, and future end on the scaffold.

Below: Tom Corbett is a lively green-eyed scryer who takes his profession seriously. "It shouldn't be easy money," he says. "If you deal with people going through an emotional crisis, this isn't funny." He complains bitterly about clients who talk while he's trying to see what the crystal shows. "It cuts across what I'm getting," he says.

Anyone who has been to an amusement park, a seashore resort, or a carnival, is familiar with the scene. The small, somewhat shabby tent. The painted stripes worn away by sun and bad weather. The sign— "Madame Za-Za, Fortunes Told"—tilted. The overall atmosphere more furtive than mysterious, more oppressive than welcoming. Instead of a tent at the seashore or on a fairground, the somewhat dismal scene could be a walk-up, one-room office in a town or city. Inside the tent or room sits

94

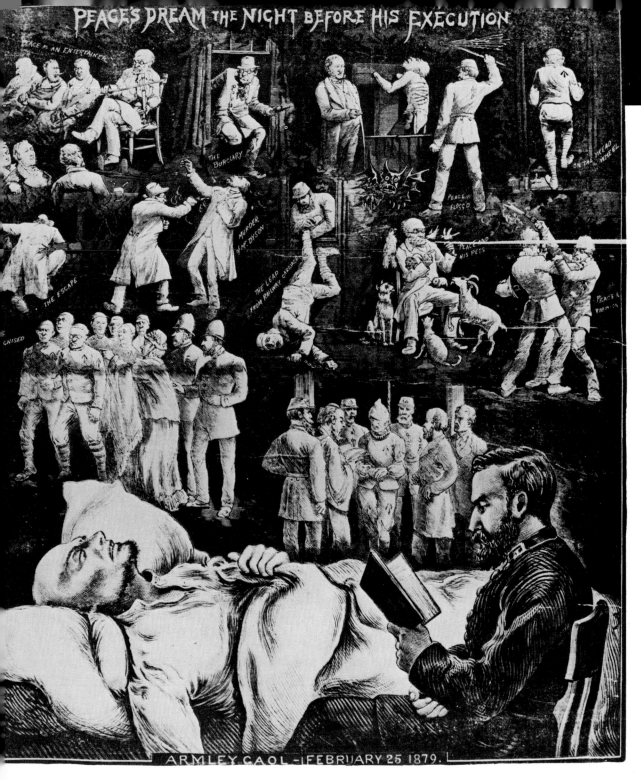

PEACE'S DREAM THE NIGHT BEFORE HIS EXECUTION

ARMLEY GAOL – FEBRUARY 25 1879.

95

# "To her the crystal is a living thing"

the *scryer*—crystal gazer. Whatever country she is to be found in, she seems to fall into one of two types: she is either positive or passive. The positive prophetess is recognizable by her dark complexion, strong features and forehead, and intent stare. She uses the crystal in front of her as if it were a living thing. When she speaks her voice is deep, penetrating, forceful. The passive prophetess is pale, and usually blue-eyed. Her voice is weak and high-pitched, and she looks into the crystal almost beseechingly, as if begging the circle of quartz to show her something, anything. Sometimes the seer—whichever type she is—wears a shawl, a beaded headscarf, and earrings to suggest the gypsy or the mystic. More often nowadays she is crisply dressed, polite, and attentive—a career woman receiving you at her place of work.

You must "cross her palm with silver," of course. Originally this was done by making the sign of a cross with a coin, but today it is likely to be by handing her some folding money. The payment made, she is ready to commence the reading. Her crystal—a word that comes from the Greek *krystallos* for "clear ice"—is shaded by a black velvet cloth, and placed in the center of the table. According to John Melville, the author of an extremely detailed manual on crystal gazing, the globe should be "$1\frac{1}{2}$ inches in diameter, or at least the size of a small orange." It should also be "enclosed in a frame of ivory, ebony, or boxwood, highly polished." Bending over the crystal, the prophetess spends a few minutes making passes with her right hand so that the surface becomes "magnetized." She then makes a series of similar passes with her left hand in order to increase the ball's sensitivity. In the stillness and silence that follows, clouds form over the crystal, and the prophetess can discern various pictures or visions in them.

Serious students of crystal gazing say that a good scryer is likely to have genuine psychic powers. But the amateur can make predictions based on general rules, even if he or she sees no pictures. For example, green or blue clouds mean joy; red, yellow, or orange ones indicate trouble. White mists are a good portent, but black cloudiness an evil one.

In fact, the globe may show her no more than her own distorted reflection. Its main purpose is to increase the seer's concentration so that she can "fix" in her mind the scenes that filter through from the future. Whether or not crystal gazers actually see the future in their globes, the controversial art of scrying is now flourishing in a way no fortune teller would have dared to foretell. Few cities throughout the world are without their quota of professional "Madam Za-Zas," and many are the communities that have an amateur scryer.

In the practice of scrying, the crystal should be kept immaculately clean. This entails regular washing with vinegar and water or fine soapsuds, and frequent polishing with a velvet cloth or chamois. No one else but its owner should handle the ball, and, when in use, the sphere should not be turned toward the light. The technique for making the sphere work is a simple one; and it has been estimated that about one person in every 20 is capable of either seeing vague shapes in the ball itself, or of having them imprinted in his or her mind. The room in which the sittings take place should preferably face north, and it should be discreetly lit with just enough light to be able to read by. No more than three people in all should be present, and the scryer should be at least an arm's length away from the other two. If they want to ask her any questions during the session, they should do so in a blank, monotonous voice so as not to disturb her concentration. They should never prompt or urge her because it will do no good. As the crystal experimenter Frederic Myers explains: "The visions do not seem to follow any law; they are a mixture of remembrances, dreams, telepathic or telestetic recognitions and precognitions. In short, crystal gazing is an empirical method of arousing *cryptesthesia* (clairvoyance); the mechanism by which this comes to pass is unknown."

What the amateurs and some of the professionals do not know is that their art was condemned in earlier times as being of "satanic origin." This was the conclusion reached in 1398 by the Faculty of Theology in Paris, which could see no difference between the scryers' crystals and the then equally prevalent onyx mirrors employed by so-called witches. Of course, it was realized that the crystal was not the only medium in which the future could be glimpsed, or in which the seeker could come into contact with the universe and the "image of God." Hindus could see the shape of things to come in ink blots or in bowls of molasses. In the West, seers among the Romans, the Arabs, and the British Druids got equal results by studying fingernails, polished stones, sword blades, soap bubbles, glasses of wine, and water. In ancient Greece, it was not uncommon to learn of people's future welfare and health by "consulting the springs." The traveler and geographer Pausanias, in his *Itinerary of Greece,* described how the fortune tellers of Patrae "tie a mirror to a fine cord, and let it down so far that it shall not plunge into the spring, but merely graze the surface of the water with its rim. Then, after praying to the goddess and burning incense, they look into the mirror, and it shows them the sick person either living or dead. So truthful is this water." Occasionally, to add to the purity of the procedure, a virgin girl or boy took the place of the scryer, who supervised the event and interpreted what the youngster saw.

By the middle of the 12th century, scrying was in fashion throughout much of Europe and most of the Middle East. It won the enthusiastic support and participation of the ordinary populace—and the condemnation of the Church. In England, the philosopher and ecclesiastic John of Salisbury, spoke out against those who looked into the future by means of "objects which are polished and shining, like a kettle of good brass, glasses, cups, and different kinds of mirrors." His admonition had little effect in his day or later. In a typical case 300 years after, a Yorkshire villager named Byg confessed to scrying as a way of discovering some of his stolen property. The charge against him was of heresy. On being found guilty, he was sentenced to march through York Cathedral with a lighted torch in·one hand, his "magical books" in the other, and a placard around his neck denouncing him as a *Sortilegus* (sooth-sayer) and *Invocator Spiritum* (invoker of spirits).

## Blood in the Crystal Ball!

Nell Montague was obliging a friend by reading the crystal for Mrs. H. in the home of her friend. When she had gazed into the crystal, a shock went all through her. There stood a tall balding man, nervously handling a revolver that he aimed at the door of the room from time to time. He talked on the phone several times, and then, as though tired of waiting for someone he may have been phoning, he pointed the gun at his own head. The crystal was diffused in blood. A woman came into the room and lifted the man's bloody head in her arms. That woman was Mrs. H!

Miss Montague didn't tell Mrs. H. all the details of her vision, but she did warn her of tragic widowhood to come soon. Mrs. H. simply laughed at this prediction, and Miss Montague was greatly relieved. However, as soon as she was alone, Miss Montague wrote down what she had seen exactly as she remembered it.

Three days after this event, on April 19, 1920, the London *Daily Mail* carried the story of the suicide of Mr. H. It said that he had been found at home "shot through the mouth, with a revolver in his right hand."

The picture in the crystal had come true.

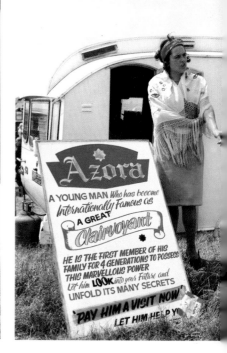

**Above:** Evadne Price, who writes the horoscopes for a London woman's magazine, is also a scryer and spiritualist. She feels that being psychic reduces her skill as an astrologer because she does not have to be a good student of the stars to tell fortunes.

Byg's offense was a minor one, however, compared with the cruel deception practiced on John Dee, a scholar who became the official fortune teller to Queen Elizabeth I. Educated at Cambridge University, Dee was a man of intellectual integrity. His research into the occult was part of his "quest for God," whom he believed could be found through alchemy, scrying, and other frowned-upon arts. His saintliness and obvious good will saved him from prosecution, and he prospered and became famous throughout Europe. Dr. Dee's mistake was in following the advice he said he had received from the Archangel Michael. This was to take a scryer called Edward Kelley as his partner, and to allow Kelley to use the crystal Dee said he had been given by the same Archangel. It was a crystal "most bright, most clear and glorious, of the bigness of an egg." He had confidence in Kelley in spite of the fact that the latter had had his ears cut off for forgery, and, in general, had a bad reputation.

After working well together for a while, Kelley told Dee that he had seen a "most wondrous and extraordinary vision." A naked 9-year-old girl named Madimi had appeared in the crystal, and had instructed Kelley that he and the good doctor should share everything they had—including their wives. At first Dee protested, and so did his wife, who considered the former apothecary's assistant "highly repulsive." By two o'clock that morning, however, Kelley had convinced the older man that Madimi must be obeyed. Reluctantly, Dee woke his wife and told her that the "cross-matching . . . must needs be done." A document of mutual sharing was signed by all four parties, and it was only torn up when Kelley suddenly lost his nerve and his temper. The partnership was dissolved, but Kelley's visions and the two scryers' experiments were recorded in the numerous volumes of Dee's diaries, which eventually came to light.

Above: John Dee was a scholar who delved into the occult as part of his "quest for God." He became the official fortune teller to Queen Elizabeth I.

Below: an engraving by a 19th-century English artist picks up an old unproved story that had been spread to discredit Dr. Dee in the early 17th century. The unfounded rumor had it that Dr. Dee dug up graves for bodies to use in trying to raise the dead.

Partly because of the shocking Dee case, partly because of exploits of charlatans, and partly through a general disenchantment with crystal gazing, scrying gradually gave way to other forms of fortune telling. It enjoyed a revival in the mid-19th century, however. This resurge of interest started when the novelist Lord Lytton, author of the much-admired *The Last Days of Pompeii,* boasted of the crystal ball he kept and consulted at his ancestral home. It got another boost when Andrew Lang, a writer and one-time president of the Society for Psychical Research, some years later had "an extraordinary experience which convinced me beyond all possible doubt about the efficacy of scrying."

In the winter of 1897, Lang was invited to dinner at a large house in his native Scotland. One of his fellow guests was an Englishman, who got into an argument about the genuineness of crystal gazing with the host's daughter, whom Lang called, "Miss Angus." The young lady challenged the scoffer to visualize a place or person of his acquaintance, and said that she would see the same person in her globe. The Englishman conjured up a ball he had recently been to, and a beautiful girl he had danced with.

"Miss Angus," wrote Lang, "then described another room, not a ballroom, comfortably furnished, in which a girl with brown hair drawn back from her forehead, and attired in a high-necked white blouse, was reading, or writing letters, under a bright light in an unshaded glass globe." A short while later the Englishman met the girl of his scrying experiment at another formal dance, and asked her what she had been doing at about 10:30 p.m. on the night of December 21. He had never seen her other than in her ball gown, had met her only once before, and knew that she and Miss Angus were total strangers. He was staggered, therefore, when the girl told him that, at the time in question, she was indeed dressed as the scryer had stated, and had been answering letters beneath just such an unshaded gas lamp.

This example is a typical one of the scryer's powers. An even more startling, but similar, case occurred in England in 1920. Sir William Barrett, a former president of the Society for Psychical Research, reported it.

It seems that a crystal gazer named Nell St. John Montague was asked by a mutual friend, identified as Mrs. R., to give a reading to a Mrs. H. Miss Montague, who had been paying a social visit to her friend's house, obligingly sent a servant to collect her crystal ball, making sure that the globe was wrapped in velvet so that the maid did not touch the quartz. Unlike most other scryers, Miss Montague had her client hold the crystal and concentrate on it as if in a trance. According to Sir William's write-up in the *Journal of the Society for Psychical Research,* Miss Montague's account was as follows: "When I took it from her hands," said the scryer, "I experienced a terrible shock . . . I warned her as delicately as I could that a gruesome tragedy was before her, an awful deed which would make her a widow almost immediately."

Mrs. H's reaction was to burst into laughter, which was a relief to the scryer. However, she made notes of what she had seen, in these words: "I can see a tall fair man, rather bald, pacing up and down a small room . . . close beside the desk is a telephone, he is excitedly taking up the receiver and speaking into it, he opens a drawer in the desk and holds an object taken from it in his right hand—it is a revolver." In Miss Montague's account, the man in the sphere twice more speaks into the phone, each time looking at the door with his gun at the ready. "With a sudden gesture," the notes go on, "he looks once more at the door and shakes his head as though giving up hope of it opening to admit someone for whom he seems to be waiting. He raises his right hand and staggers back, the revolver is now pointing at his own head—then I see blood everywhere gushing. A woman comes into the room, the same woman who is in the room with me now, only in the picture she wears a loose wrapper, she lifts his head—blood is everywhere."

Three days later, Mrs. H.'s husband committed suicide exactly as Miss Montague had described. However, the scryer helped save the life of a man who might have been killed by Mr. H. This was the husband of Mrs. R., the friend who had originally introduced Mrs. H. and Miss Montague. On the day of Mr. H.'s suicide, Mr. R. visited the scryer in a great hurry. He said he had a message from his wife to go at once to see Mr. H., who "wanted to take him [Mr. R.] with him." Remembering the vision in the crystal, Miss Montague managed to delay Mr. R. for about 15 minutes. According to Mr. R., he afterward went to the H.'s home, and, as he rang the doorbell, heard a shot. Shortly after, he was told that Mr. H. had shot himself. Upon learning about Miss Montague's forecast, he realized he was the person Mr. H. seemed intent on shooting in the vision—to take someone with him in death. "I owe my life to Miss Montague's warning," he is reported as saying.

Cases such as this restored much of its former popularity and following to scrying. A. E. Waite, the occult historian, commended it as "undoubtedly one of the most innocent, pleasing, and successful methods of minor magical practice." Attending a scrying session can be compared to going to the movies—the difference being that instead of watching a sequence of pictures about the lives of fictitious characters, you are viewing an excerpt or trailer from your own life to come. If this is so, then dreams must be our own private movies, produced for and screened each night to an audience of one— ourselves.

Not everyone appreciates this fact, and one of the most widespread fallacies about dreams is that not everybody has them. We all know the person who boasts, "Dreams? Never had one in my life. When I go to bed I sleep"! The view that dreamless sleep was possible was long accepted, despite the philosopher Immanuel Kant's statement toward the end of the 18th century that "there is no sleep without dreams," and the similar claims of modern psychologists. Then, in 1952, a scientist suddenly noticed that babies' eyes sporadically moved under their closed lids when they were asleep. This observation led to a new approach to sleep investigation, and research later showed that the movements—called REMs—take place some-

## Caught by The Crystal!

Dr. Edmund Waller, an Englishman living in Paris in the early 1900s, was having a sleepless night. He wandered downstairs, and, finding the crystal his father had just bought, gazed idly into it. There, to his surprise, he saw the image of Mme. D., whom he had promised to look after during her husband's out-of-town journey.

The next day, Waller again looked into the crystal, and again saw Mme. D.—with a man. He rubbed his eyes, and looked still again. The pair remained in view, this time at a racecourse outside Paris. Agitated by all these visions, Waller went to the racecourse next day—and there met Mme. D. with a man whom he took to be the one he had seen in the crystal.

Waller continued to see Mme. D., her husband, and the other man in the crystal. One scene showed the illicit lovers in a particular Paris restaurant. On the husband's return, Waller told him about the visions. The two men went to the restaurant revealed by the crystal, and there found Mme. D. with her lover.

There was a tragic aftermath to Waller's visions: Mme. D. ended in an asylum, a broken woman after her husband had divorced her.

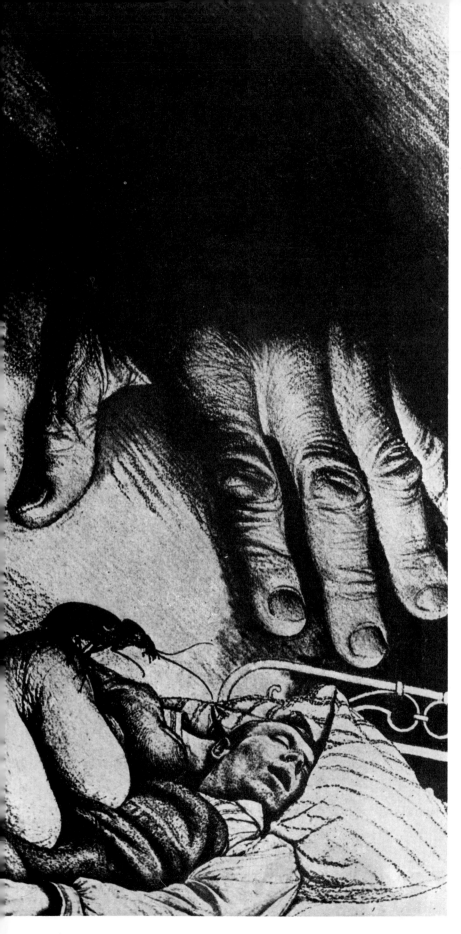

Above: an engraving of 1878 is fittingly entitled "Preparing for a Nightmare." Eating pork pie and pickles, and reading lurid tales before bedtime is asking for it. Left: this drawing graphically shows the horror of a bad dream.

Below: Freud said that dreams guard sleep. He illustrated this theory by showing how a nurse-maid wakes up to her charge's cries only after a dream, in which he urinates a sea full, has helped her stay asleep for a time.

time during the sleep of all humans. It was established that REMs indicate dreaming; that every man, woman, and child has from five to seven REM periods a night at hourly intervals; and that dreams take up one-third of the sleeping time of adults. These findings were also borne out by Dr. Charles Fisher of Mount Sinai Hospital, New York, who stated that: "If a sleeper is awakened in the middle of a dream, he will make up the final sequence at the next opportunity."

As dream statistics began to mount up, it was calculated that some 730 billion dreams are dreamed each year in the USA. This information added to the already impressive data compiled on dreams, which included their role in *oneiromancy* (forecasting the future from dreams), and the number of times they had signposted or warned of coming events. Among the oldest recorded prophetic dreams are those in the Bible—the most famous being that of the Egyptian Pharaoh who dreamt that seven fat cows were eaten by seven lean cows, and seven ripe ears of corn were devoured by seven lean ears. Joseph, the captive slave who interpreted the dream, firmly stated that Egypt was due for seven years of plenty followed by seven years of famine. "God," he announced, "has shown Pharaoh what He is about to do."

That God was not averse to revealing His intentions in dreams, and that it was not sacrilegious to act upon His warnings, was confirmed by St. Thomas Aquinas. His writings have been called the "cornerstone of the Roman Catholic Church." In his *Summa Theologica* he acknowledged that "divination by dreams is not unlawful. It is the experience of all men that a dream contains some indication of the future. Therefore, it is vain to deny that dreams have efficacy in divination." Humans believed this as far back as 650 B.C. when King Assurbanipal of Assyria filled his library with clay tablets bearing the meanings of dreams. People still believed it in A.D. 150 when the Roman soothsayer Artemidorus of Daldis compiled his manual of dream interpretation. This manual was read and followed for the next thousand years.

By then, scholars were pondering which was the true reality— the dream state or the waking condition. This philosophical puzzle had been posed as early as the 3rd century B.C. by the Taoist mystic Chuang Tzu, who asked on waking from a dream in which he was a butterfly: "Am I Chuang Tzu who dreamed he was a butterfly, or a butterfly now dreaming I am Chuang Tzu?" His question was repeated by the 17th-century French mathematician and devotional author Blaise Pascal, who queried: "Who knows that when we think we are awake we may not be in slumber, from which slumber we awaken when we sleep?" The quandary was echoed by other philosophers, and in order to experience such fantasies and/or realities, ascetics would deliberately induce dreams of revelation by fasting, denying the appetites of the body, and making their beds in temples and sacred buildings.

They sought proof of the existence of afterlife, and declared that the symbols of dreams—no matter how obscure or mystifying—were meant to be revealing. For the less mystical person, some dreams were so clear, so vivid, so concrete that

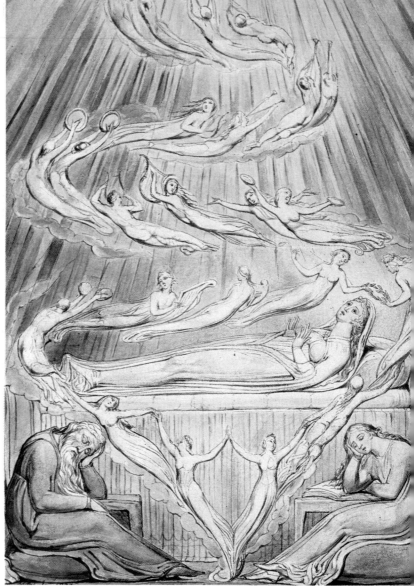

Right: the English visionary William Blake was also a painter and poet. He was fascinated with the symbolism of dreams, and was frequently inspired by them. This painting, "Queen Katherine's Dream," is typical of his fantasy.

Below: a 13th-century painting of the Bible story about Pharaoh's dream of seven fat and seven lean cows. After others failed, the young Jew Joseph interpreted it.

they were far more disturbing than those cluttered with symbolism. One such person was the 19th-century French dream researcher Alfred Maury, who believed he had been taken back in time when he had a vivid dream in which the entire course of the French Revolution was paraded before him. In the dream, he was one of the participants in the uprising, and, on being accused of "crimes against the people" was sentenced to be guillotined. He was kneeling before the instrument when the bedpost suddenly broke and fell on the back of his neck.

Even more frightening than this was the dream of President Abraham Lincoln a short time before his assassination at Ford's theater in Washington, D.C. A skeptical man who dismissed the authenticity of biblical dreams, he nevertheless discussed his own "sleep premonition" with his wife and several of their friends. According to Lincoln, he had gone to bed tired one night after reading some dispatches from his generals. He soon began to dream and heard "subdued sobs, as if a number of people were weeping." In the dream he left his bed, went downstairs in the White House, and walked through a series of empty rooms until the sobbing led him into the East Room. There he met with a "sickening surprise." "Before me," he recounted, "was a catafalque, on which rested a corpse wrapped in funeral vestments. Around it were stationed soldiers who were acting as guards; and there was a throng of people, some gazing mournfully upon the corpse, whose face was covered, others weeping pitifully." Worried, Lincoln approached one of the soldiers and demanded to know who was dead. 'The President,' was his answer, 'he was killed by an assassin!' Then came a loud burst of grief from the crowd which awoke me from my dream."

A similar "death dream" featuring a head of state had come to a mining engineer in Cornwall, England on May 3, 1812. The engineer, John Williams, also related the "dreadful nightmare" to his wife, telling her that he dreamt he was in the lobby of the House of Commons in London. "A small man, dressed in a blue coat and a white waistcoat, entered, and immediately, I saw a person whom I had observed on my first entrance, dressed in a snuff-colored coat with metal buttons, take a pistol from under his coat and present it at the little man above-mentioned. The pistol was discharged, and the ball entered under the left breast of the person at whom it was directed. I saw the blood issue from the place where the ball had struck him, his countenance instantly altered, and he fell to the ground. Upon enquiry whom the sufferer might be, I was informed he was the Chancellor."

At the time the prime minister, Spencer Perceval, was also the chancellor of the exchequer, and Williams' wife and friends were convinced that it was the prime minister who had figured in his dream. So strong was their conviction that Williams debated whether or not to go to London to warn Perceval of his imminent death. However, after talking it over some more, he decided to remain at home and save himself exposure to "contempt and vexation." For the next few days he anxiously studied the newspapers as they arrived with the post. "On the evening of May 13th," he wrote later, "no account of Mr. Perceval's death was in the newspapers, but my second son, returning from Truro, [a town in Cornwall] came into the room where I was sitting and exclaimed, 'Oh father, your dream has come true! Mr. Perceval has been shot in the lobby of the House of Commons; there is an account come from London to Truro written after the newspapers were printed.' The fact was that Mr. Perceval was assassinated on the evening of the 11th."

Such stories—which have been authenticated as far as is possible—fit into none of the categories or explanations offered by most men of science. To them, dreams have definite causes and occasional effects, but little or nothing to do with coming events. Sigmund Freud described dreams as "the royal road to the Unconscious," and felt that they were basically wish fulfillment. He agreed with the Latin poet Lucretius that dreams dealt with daytime interests and waking life, so that a man who was hungry might dream of food. Likewise, if the blankets were too heavy, the sleeper might dream he was being engulfed by quicksand, and if he were sexually frustrated, he would

## Dreams for Sale

This 18th-century engraving shows a London street peddler with her dream books for sale. People always want to know what their dreams mean, and they buy all kinds of books to help interpret them. Here are some interpretations from a dream book of 19th-century England:

*Ants*—a dream about ants means that you will move to a large city and have a big family of boys; it also implies wealth, but only if you are industrious.

*Earwig*—if this creature enters your dream, it indicates that you have an enemy working against you in secret. Beware of a small person with light brown hair!

*Flying*—this means that the dreamer has an aspiration he will never reach, and he had better change his course immediately or he will end up in ruin.

*Ink*—black ink in a dream foretells involvement in some disgraceful scheme; red ink tells of good news.

*Whistling*—to dream that you are whistling popular songs denotes that you can't carry even the simplest and easiest tune.

build up a sexual fantasy. Freud greatly stressed the importance of the sexual basis of dreams. He was criticized for this by his former disciple, the psychologist Alfred Adler, who believed that dreams were a "rehearsal" of man's drive for power, which renewed itself daily.

To the Swiss psychologist Carl Jung, the third outstanding figure in the new Age of Psychology, dreams had neither a sexual nor a power-seeking connotation. To him, they were a kind of receptacle or storehouse of all the memories, reflections, and impressions that had been passed on to man throughout the centuries by his earliest ancestors. Like Adler, he broke away from Freud to form his own school. This gave him a new attitude toward his patients, and a less rigid and dogmatic method of dream analysis. His aim, he explained, was to leave things to chance. As a result, his patients spontaneously reported their dreams and fantasies to him, and he merely asked, "What occurs to you in connection with that?" or, "How do you mean that?" Said Jung: "The interpretations seemed to follow of their own accord from the patients' replies and associations. I avoided all theoretical points of view, and simply helped the patients to understand the dream-images by themselves, without application to rules and theories."

Certainly as far as creative artists are concerned, it seems better to allow them to indulge in interpretation or analysis of their dreams, and to put their night visions into print. For example, dreams were in part responsible for three of the greatest horror novels in Western literature—*Frankenstein,*

Above: the killing of British Prime Minister Spencer Perceval in 1812 was the subject of a dream by a Cornish miner. The dream was exactly like the real murder— but came nine days ahead of time. Below: ten days before a political murder of a British military officer by Irish nationals in 1922, a friend of the murdered man foresaw his death by assassination in a dream.

*The Strange Case of Dr. Jekyll and Mr. Hyde,* and *Dracula.* Frankenstein's creation led the ghoulish parade of literary monsters. The story came out of a dream by Mary Shelley in 1818. Some 70 years later, the novelist Robert Louis Stevenson had a dream that terrified his wife, but inspired him. "My husband's cries of horror caused me to arouse him," she recorded, "much to his indignation. 'I was dreaming a fine bogey tale,'" he said reproachfully. The next morning Stevenson went to his desk and started on the first draft of his nightmarish tale of Dr. Jekyll's dual personality. The following decade, in the 1890s, the author Bram Stoker went to bed after "eating generously" of cold crab meat at supper, and had a nightmare in which Count Dracula first bared his fangs to start a long and notorious career.

A contemporary writer who profited from a predictive dream is T. E. B. Clarke, whose screenplay for *The Lavender Hill Mob* won him an Oscar in 1951. He didn't write a novel about his racing dream, but he enjoyed telling it. It happened when he was a 15-year-old schoolboy in 1922. "I was sitting in a tea-shop," he writes, "when a newsboy entered holding an evening paper with 'Derby Result' on it. I bought a paper and looked at the Stop Press. The first three were there, but on waking I could remember only the winner's name—Manna. . . . Two

**Below: the tutor of a noble had a dream in which his pupil was killed. He tried and failed to warn of possible danger. The tutor was Bishop Joseph Lanyi, and the noble was Austrian Archduke Franz Ferdinand. The assassination of the archduke thrust the world into war in 1914.**

## President Lincoln's Prophetic Dream

On an April night in 1865— with the trials of the Civil War still heavy on his mind— President Abraham Lincoln lay asleep and dreaming. In his dream, he was asleep in his huge bed in the White House. Suddenly he was wakened by sobbing. Getting up and following the sound of the weeping, Lincoln found himself in the East Room. There he saw people filing past a catafalque guarded by soldiers. The men and women were paying their last respects to a body laid in state.

The face of the corpse was covered from Lincoln's view, but he could see that those present were deeply affected by the person's death. Finally, he went to one of the soldiers and asked who was dead. "The President," was the answer. "He was killed by an assassin." With that horrifying reply came a loud outcry of grief from the group near the catafalque—and Lincoln woke up.

This troubling dream, which Lincoln told his wife Mary and several of their friends, turned out to be a prophetic one. In that very month, Lincoln went to the theater for a rare night away from his pressing responsibilities. Awaiting him there instead of a night of pleasure was a fatal bullet from an assassin's gun.

These photographs reenact a murder committed in 19th-century England, and known as the Red Barn Mystery. It involved the killing of a girl by a farmer, who buried her under the floor of a red barn. The man then wrote regularly to the girl's parents to allay suspicion. Months later, however, the girl's mother three times dreamed of her daughter's death—just as it happened. She insisted on taking up the barn floor—and solved the mystery.

years later I was thrilled to see Manna among the entries for a two-year-old race. I knew then that he was destined to win the Derby the following year . . . Manna duly won the Derby at 9-to-1. The horse had probably not even been born when I had my dream."

Similar though more serious experiences have been recorded by leading scientists. The Nobel Prize-winning Danish physicist Niels Bohr stated that his revolutionary atomic model first came to him in a dream, and the German mathematician Karl Gauss admitted having dreamt rather than discovered his laws of induction. The chemist Paul Ehrlich—who shared the 1908 Nobel Prize for medicine—made no secret of the fact that his side chain theory was "mainly the result of a dream." Con-

fronted with the statements of such men, it is difficult for even the most cynical to dismiss the importance and significance of dreams.

The one thing we can be sure of is the overriding physical importance of dreams. In the words of the occult author and diplomat Benjamin Walker: "A person who is not allowed to dream while asleep will start dreaming when he is awake. The hypertense dream-psyche will burst through the waking consciousness, and he will live in a dream world, the world of the psychotic and the disoriented. Continued dream deprivation will bring mental collapse, and may eventually lead to death." Which is another way of saying that we don't live to dream, but dream to live.

**Above: a contemporary engraving of the red barn in which Maria Marten was murdered in 1827.**

# 7

# Nostradamus and After

It is midnight and the astrologer mounts the spiral staircase to his secret study at the top of the house. He knows that he will not be disturbed there, and that his wife will keep any unwelcome visitors away from him. He sits before a three-legged brass stool, lays down his laurel wand between its legs, and proceeds to sprinkle the hem of his robe and his feet with water. For a moment he feels frightened before the power he is about to evoke. Then his courage returns, he places a bowl of water on the stool, and peers silently into the liquid. After a while the power "speaks" to him,

Above: this early 18th-century engraving shows Catherine de Medicis, queen of France from 1547 to 1589, getting a preview of future rulers by means of mirror prediction. With her in the engraving is Nostradamus, her adviser and confidant.

Right: the obscure rhymed predictions of the French astrologer Nostradamus have puzzled and interested the world for about 400 years. This early engraving shows him busy at his stargazing.

Predictions Véritables et
Remarquables
Centuries
de Michel
Nostradamus

# "Pictures of future war, famine, earthquake, fire, and disaster"

It is thought that several of the well-known Nostradamus prophecies refer to Napoleon. The following verse is one example:
"Of a name which never was held by a French king,
Never was there so fearful a thunderbolt.
Italy, Spain, and the English tremble.
He will be greatly attentive to foreign women."
The translation and interpretation of this four-line verse is the work of Erika Cheetham, English author of a recent book on the ancient prophecies. According to this author, it applies to Napoleon as follows: he was the first Bonaparte, a new name among French rulers; he was bold and powerful (a thunderbolt); all European nations came to fear him; and he was in love with three foreign women.

and he is "divinely possessed." The water becomes cloudy, and he sees therein visions of the future—pictures of war, famine, earthquake, fire, and disaster. Lighting a taper, he then goes into a trance, in which his travel into future time increases in range and detail. All the while, as the voices from space go on, and the images appear in the water, he writes down his visions in a thick vellum book. His activity lasts until dawn. Then, with the first light, he hears and sees no more. He leans back in his chair, exhausted. Downstairs, his wife will soon be preparing breakfast. In a little while he will join her, eat with her, tell her of the revelations he has seen, and rest until it is time for his labors of divination to start again the following midnight.

All this sounds somewhat like an old-fashioned melodrama, but it was serious business to the man involved in it—the French physician and astrologer Michel de Notredame, known as Nostradamus. To him, there was nothing absurd in what he did and what he saw and heard. To him, it was the natural way —the only way—in which he could, as he put it, "leave a memorial of me after my death, to the common benefit of mankind, concerning the things which the Divine Essence has revealed to me by astronomical revelations."

Nostradamus wrote these words in a dedication to his son in the first edition of his famous *Centuries,* published in Lyons in March 1555. In his work, *centuries* do not refer to periods of a hundred years, but to a series of prophecies numbering 100 to a section. Although the prophecies came to Nostradamus with complete clarity, he did not present them clearly to his readers. Both in order not to offend the Church and to reduce the possibility of mass alarm among the general populace, he wrote his prophecies in four-line rhymes of obscure and symbolic language.

A noted scholar, Nostradamus wrote his verses in a mixture of puns, anagrams (Paris, for example, was written *Ripas*), French, Latin, and a language of his own making. "If I came to refer to that which will be in the future," he explained, "those of the realm, sect, religion, and faith would find it so poorly in accord with their petty fancies that they would come to condemn that which future ages shall know and understand to be true." In a letter to his patron, King Henry II of France—whose death, incidentally, he correctly predicted—Nostradamus added: "Some may answer that the rhyme is as easy to understand as to blow one's nose, but the sense is more difficult to grasp."

Astrology was then at one of its peaks, not to enjoy so much popularity again until the 1930s. In spite of this, Nostradamus was suspected of being in league with the Devil. A virtuous God-fearing man who had been known to burn occult books that went against the canons of the Church, the astrologer quoted the Bible in his defense, from Matthew vii. 6: "Such alone as are inspired by the divine power can predict particular events in a spirit of prophecy." His own "divine virtue and inspiration," he claimed, came directly from God the Creator, who used him as a spokesman for His own plans and intentions for the future.

Employing a blend of learning and intuition, Nostradamus

concentrated mainly on *facts* about the future, rather than *dates*. He even got the date of his own death wrong, dying in July 1566 instead of November 1567, as he had predicted. However, it did not affect the success of the *Centuries*, which went from edition to edition, and which has been in print from his day to this—about 400 years running.

His nocturnal methods of divination were based largely on an ancient book called *De Mysteriis Egyptorum*, an edition of which was published in Lyons in 1547. Its author, the 4th-century Greek philosopher Iamblichus, stressed the importance of dressing in robes and using a wand and a three-legged stool. To later disciples of Nostradamus, such trappings heightened the impact of his predictions.

Here is a translation of the third verse of Nostradamus' *Century One*:

> *When the litters are overturned by the whirlwind and faces are covered by cloaks, the new republic will be troubled by its people. At this time the reds and the whites will rule wrongly.*

This has been interpreted as a forecast of the French Revolution of 1789, and the coming of what Nostradamus called the Common Advent, or the assumption of power by the ordinary man. The "reds" and the "whites" was taken to refer to the era of Robespierre and the Terror, white being the color of the Bourbon rulers who were overthrown, and red the color of the Revolutionaries. One of his few predictions with a definite date also anticipates the French Revolution. In a letter to King

Overleaf: Nostradamus was one prophet of the long line that warned of the end of the world. Interpreters of his riddle-like, rhymed predictions say he foresaw the world's destruction near the year 2000. John Martin, a British artist who lived in the last century, may or may not have known about the prophetic astrologer. However, his powerful painting could almost be said to be a rendering of Nostradamus' vision of the final, horrible holocaust.

**The Duke and Duchess of Windsor just after their wedding. Interpreters of Nostradamus say he foresaw King Edward VIII's abdication for love of a divorcee. Erika Cheetham refers to a verse mentioning "divorce" and "king of the islands" as the prophecy.**

Henry II on June 27, 1558, Nostradamus foretold an uprising against the Church, stating: "It shall be in the year 1792, at which time everyone will think it a renovation of the age." As it happened, the Republic of France—born and bred out of anticlerical thinking—came into being in September 1792. The year before that saw the flight of King Louis XVI and Queen Marie-Antoinette when, as the astrologer prophesied, they traveled by a "circuitous route" at night before being captured by the mob and beheaded.

It seemed only natural that, as a Frenchman, some of Nostradamus' most successful prophecies should concern his own country. In verse seven of *Century One*, he speaks of "letters intercepted on their way," a prediction that could apply to the celebrated case of Captain Alfred Dreyfus 339 years later. In this case of anti-Semitism that divided the country, the innocent Dreyfus was unjustly convicted on the basis of intercepted letters said to have been sent by him to the Germans. Before getting a public pardon, Dreyfus had a review of his case by an official named Rousseau, as Nostradamus foretold. This minister was so bitterly anti-Dreyfus that he found the officer guilty a second time, even though Dreyfus was soon after fully exonerated.

These predictions were followed by a vision of the atrocities in the city of Nantes in 1793, when 1000 citizens opposed to the Revolutionaries were either guillotined or drowned naked in the river Loire—"Cries, groans at Nantes pitiful to see," were the words of Nostradamus. Napoleon comes in for a number of prophecies, including his birth ("an emperor will be born near Italy who will cost the empire dear"), his retreat from fire-torn Moscow in the winter of 1812–13 ("A mass of men will draw

**Above: the Great Fire of London in 1666 seems to be clearly predicted by Nostradamus in these first two lines of one of his rhymes, as translated and interpreted by Erika Cheetham: "The blood of the just will be demanded of London Burnt by fire in three times twenty plus six."**

**Left: the young Marconi looks proud and confident in this 1895 photograph of him with his first wireless transmitter. Evidence that Nostradamus predicted radio and electricity is given by Erika Cheetham from this prophecy: "When the animal tamed by man Begins to speak after great efforts and difficulty, The lightning so harmful to the rod Will be taken from the earth and suspended in the air."**

near . . . the Destroyer will ruin the old city"), and his defeat at Waterloo in 1815 when the Leopard (England) and the Boar (Prussia) crushed the Eagle (Napoleon).

As he said himself, however, Nostradamus had foreknowledge of more than just one country or one continent. Some of his most fascinating forecasts concern the United States, its inhabitants, and its political leaders. Three times in the ten books of the *Centuries* are mentions such as "the great man . . . struck down in the day by a thunderbolt"; "the great one will fall"; "the world put into trouble by three brothers; their enemies will seize the marine city, hunger, fire, blood, plague, and all evils doubled." These references are generally taken as a warning of the assassination of President John F. Kennedy, a presentiment of the gunning down of his brother, Robert, and a hint that the troubles of Senator Edward Kennedy would be ongoing. The destruction of New York appears to be foreseen by the astrologer in three references stating the "earthshaking fire [which] will cause tremors around the New City"; "the sky will burn at 45 degrees, fire approaches the Great New City"; and the "King will want to enter the New City."

Apart from the devastation and/or invasion of New York, Nostradamus predicted that the whole of the USA would be involved in a cataclysmic third world war. This would be started by China, and would end with a sky filled with "weapons and rockets" with tremendous damage "inflicted on the left" (in this case, the Western Hemisphere). What makes this particular prophecy more chilling than most is how his verse six of *Century Two* apparently describes the atom bomb attacks on Nagasaki and Hiroshima in 1945:

*Near the harbor and in two cities will be two scourges, the like of which have never been seen. Hunger, plague within, people thrown out by the sword will cry for help from the great immortal God.*

Predating this in time—although not in the *Centuries* themselves, which are not chronological—is his line about "fire in the ruined ships of the West." This has been interpreted as the blazing American vessels and battleships during the Japanese attack on Pearl Harbor in December 1941. As for England, in *Century Ten* the astrologer anticipated the abdication of King Edward VIII, who gave up his throne to marry the twice-divorced American woman, Wallis Simpson. "The young born to the realm of Britain, which his dying father had commended to him . . . London will dispute with him, and the kingdom will be demanded back from the son."

By the time of his death, Nostradamus had predicted such unrelated and varied events as the victory of General Charles de Gaulle to gain the leadership of France, the Hungarian Revolution of 1956, the death of Hitler in his Berlin bunker, the collapse of the French Maginot Line in World War II, and the influenza epidemic that swept through the world in 1918-19—"the pestilence" following the "dreadful war."

The work of Nostradamus was not formally condemned by a Papal Court until 1781, when it was put on the Index of prohibited books. By then, the visionary's influence and example had built up a following among both the clerical and the secular. One of the most remarkable of the prophets who came after Nostradamus was the 18th-century poet Jacques Cazotte, whose pleasant manners and modest talents were enough to gain him a place in French high society of the day. His most famous recorded prophecy took place on a summer's evening in 1788, toward the end of a garden party given by the Duchess de Gramont. As a protégé of his hostess, Cazotte's principal purpose at such gatherings was to read his latest sonnets or odes. This he usually did in mild, gentle tones. On this particular occasion, however, the poet showed the sharp side of his nature and talent. It came when Guillaume des Malesherbes, one of Louis XVI's ministers, proposed a toast to "the day when reason shall triumph in the affairs of men—even though I shall not live to see that day."

Cazotte swung round on him, and his party mask dropped. "On the contrary, sir," he exclaimed. "You *will* live to see the day—to your cost! It shall come in five years time with a great French Revolution!"

While the guests stood open-mouthed around him, Cazotte turned to several other highly placed politicians and courtiers, and told them what their fates would be. The King's favorite, Chamfort, would join his friend Malesherbes on the guillotine, he predicted; the Marquis de Condorcet would "cheat the

**Above: this somewhat allegorical view of the execution of King Charles I of England in 1649 was done by an artist of the period. The Nostradamus rhyme put forward as a prophecy of this event speaks of a fortress near the Thames River, a king locked up inside, and the death of the king.**

**Left: the rise of Oliver Cromwell, shown here, meant the fall of Charles I after the English Civil War. The prophetic rhyme supposed to foretell this event talks of a man who was "born of obscure rank" in England, and who was to "gain empire through force." Cromwell was of a humble family, and became the English ruler after the Civil War.**

executioner" by taking poison; as for the Duchess herself, she would "ride to the scaffold in a woodcutter's cart." As the shock gradually wore off, the aristocrats began to snigger self-defensively among themselves. Then one of the company—an atheist named Jean La Harpe, who later wrote an account of the evening—stepped forward.

"What of me, Monsieur Cazotte?" he asked mockingly. "Don't tell me that I, of all people, am not destined for the guillotine!"

Cazotte smiled at him. "You are not, sir," he replied, "but only so that you can undergo an even more horrible fate. For you, Monsieur Atheist, are to become a devout and happy Christian!"

The laughter at this was even louder. But Cazotte had the final, I-told-you-so laugh. Everything came about as he had said it would, and La Harpe—whose conversion to Christianity was one of the sensations of the day—bequeathed his manuscript about Cazotte and his "ridiculous predictions" to the monastery in which he had become a man of God.

The prediction of the violent end of Louis XVI remained the outstanding example of predictive powers in the world until the morning of May 13, 1917. On that day, three small children were quietly herding sheep in the hills near the village of Fatima in central Portugal. Ten-year-old Lucia dos Santos and her cousins Jacinta, aged seven, and Francisco, nine, suddenly saw two dazzling flashes of light. The illumination came from a stubby oak tree nearby. Suspended in the center of the "ball of light" was the figure of a beautiful woman. As the youngsters

**Miracle healer and clairvoyant, Edgar Cayce was one of the most famous psychic figures of recent times. According to his own records, he diagnosed and treated some 30,000 patients. He worked while in a trance state, and, sometimes, from hundreds of miles away. In 1936, Cayce had a prophetic dream about vast upheaval in the world, in which much of the United States was destroyed.**

stiffened and gazed at her, she told them not to be afraid. "I will not harm you," she said as she became indistinct and gradually faded away.

Her last words were to ask the children to return to the spot on the 13th of each month until October, at which time a great and dreadful secret would be revealed to them. Despite a beating they received from their parents for "telling lies," Lucia and her cousins—together with some 50 inquisitive villagers—were back on the hill at noon on June 13. The children knelt and said their rosaries, and the beautiful lady radiated into view from the east, like a "glowing messenger from God." This time her message was not so encouraging. She asserted that Jacinta and Francisco would soon be "called to Heaven," and that Lucia would live only in order to spread the Madonna's message. At this, the belief grew that the luminous visitor was the Virgin Mary.

The Virgin Mary's next appearance was on July 13. Before an audience of more than 5000 people—of whom only Lucia, Jacinta, and Francisco could actually see her—she warned of a coming catastrophe that would be even greater than World War I, and that would destroy the world. The first sign of the disaster would be seen in the heavens—"a bright, unknown light which will be God's sign that he is about to punish the people of the world for their crimes." Once again the three children were beaten—and even imprisoned. The charge was taking God's name in vain—as well as scaring the souls out of the adults in the village.

However, the children's persistence impressed everyone. In addition, the story of a similar vision that had appeared to two little shepherdesses in La Salette, France in 1846, created more interest and a tendency to belief. Therefore, some 80,000 spectators converged on Fatima on October 13 to watch Lucia receive her briefing on humanity's fate. Like the Madonna of La Salette, the Fatima Virgin spoke of "vast destruction by disease and fire . . . Nature will protest at the evil done by men and earthquakes will occur in protest." As she spoke—again only to Lucia and her companions—the sky was streaked and spattered with color like a giant palette. The sun nose-dived toward earth, then flattened out and rose again. Vivid shadows flitted over the ground. The onlookers prostrated themselves in terror, crying out to God to spare them. But the children remained calm and in command of themselves.

Not long afterward, Jacinta and Francisco died in the post-World War I flu epidemic said to have been forecast by Nostradamus. As a result of her experiences—and to escape from the publicity that was turning her into a sideshow freak—Lucia decided to become a nun. She entered a convent school and became a novice in the fall of 1926. Adopting the name of Sister Marie das Dores (Sister Mary of the Sorrows), she prepared to receive future warnings from on high. In 1927, she claimed that Christ himself had visited her, and that he had asked her to be ready for "the Lady's" final and most momentous message of all—which would be imparted to her some time in the year 1960.

Before that date arrived, something happened that seemed

to be a fulfillment of Lucia's earlier visions. On the night of January 25, 1938, the Aurora Borealis, or Northern Lights, was visible throughout western Europe. The bright streams of green, violet, yellow, and flaming red that forked like lightning in the sky made many people think of the words of the Madonna 21 years earlier, when she spoke to Lucia of the "bright light by night." In 1960—the year Lucia said she would get the Virgin's final message—she was cloistered in the Portuguese convent of Coimbra. Thousands of Catholics throughout the world demanded to know what the Madonna had said to her. But Lucia now aged 53, was not talking. She did not reveal her secret until 1967, and then only to Pope Paul VI.

It is still not known what she said to the Pope— whether she confessed that her story had been a fake all along, or whether he felt that her prophecy was too frightening, too extreme to be made known to mankind. Whatever it was that she whispered to the Pope, it was said that he turned white and swung away from her.

Had the message concerned the inevitability of World War III—which is a possibility—it coincided not only with the major predictions of Nostradamus, but also with those of the renowned American clairvoyant Edgar Cayce (pronounced Casey). Called the "sleeping prophet," Cayce was best-known as a faith healer. Born on a Kentucky farm in March 1877, he was also a visionary, much in the manner of William Blake or the Swedish theologian Emanuel Swedenborg. Cayce first spoke to his "vision visitors" at the age of six. By his death in 1945, he had predicted such things as laser beams, the discovery of the Dead Sea Scrolls, the Wall Street crash of 1929, and the earthquakes, hurricanes, and tidal waves that struck California, Japan, and the Philippines respectively in 1926.

Like Nostradamus, Cayce was deeply religious. A daily reader of the Bible, he believed that he was merely an instrument through which the Almighty channeled his cosmic information. Of the 8000 trancelike readings that he gave over a period of 43 years, none had more influence or significance than his prophecies about a third world war, due to start around 1999, and the end of civilization as we know it shortly after A.D. 2000. He saw the end of the world in a dream in which he was reborn in 2100 in Nebraska, and flew over a desolated United States in an odd-shaped metal aircraft. He also foresaw the total destruction of Los Angeles and San Francisco along with much of the western part of the country.

His vision of the future—as gloomy as any in the doom-laden history of divination—took place in 1936. It dealt with more than just the usual devastation coming out of the sky— the "darts in the sky" that Nostradamus wrote of when prophesying the final war between East and West. To Cayce, there was also danger from below. It came from the submerged and mythical continent of Atlantis, which has allegedly been lying beneath the waters of the Atlantic as a lost civilization for some 12,000 years.

According to Cayce, Atlantis was the original Eden, the first place on Earth in which "man changed his spiritual for his physical form." Because of man's self-destructive inhumanity,

## Where Once Stood New York City...

Edgar Cayce, one of the best-known seers and faith healers of this century, had a cosmic vision in 1936. In it, he was reborn in the year 2100 with the knowledge that he had been Edgar Cayce from 1877 to 1945. With the scientists who were investigating his story, he flew across North America in an odd-shaped aircraft at fantastic speed. They landed among the ruins of a huge city, which was in the process of being rebuilt, and asked what the name of it was. "New York City," came the startling reply.

Along with the vision of a devastated New York, Cayce foresaw violent changes in all of the United States and the world. Nebraska had become the west coast after earthquakes had shattered the rest of the west—including Los Angeles and San Francisco— and Alabama was partly under water. Much of Japan, too, was submerged, and northern Europe had been completely altered by chaotic upheavals. During the cataclysmic changes, new lands had appeared from beneath both the Atlantic and Pacific oceans. With this vision, Cayce joined the prophets who have foretold of vast destruction throughout the world around the year 2000.

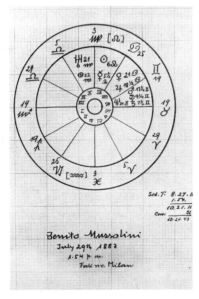

**Above: astrologer Louis de Wohl was on the payroll of the British government during World War II. He was hired to check on what advice might be given the Germans by their official astrologers. Below: this is Mussolini's horoscope as cast by de Wohl in 1941. De Wohl rightly predicted that the Italian dictator would meet "a violent and sudden end."**

went Cayce's prediction, he has been sentenced to extinction by the reemergence of Atlantis, whose inhabitants were the first possessors of death rays, atomic bombs, and machine-minds. Before this comes about, however, Communism will have been destroyed. Again like Nostradamus, Cayce feared the growth and increasing power of Marxism. (In *Century Nine*, Nostradamus warns that "the anti-Czar will exterminate everyone.") Cayce, however, believed that the attempt to "level not only the economic life but also the mental and spiritual welfare as well, will not last very long." He adds: "When one forgets to love one's neighbor, the Lord cannot have clemency, and such a situation cannot continue."

While time sped toward the day of reckoning set by Cayce for 2000, a simple old Italian woman, Mamma Rosa, was being honored by the latest visitations from the Virgin. In the two years between 1965 and 1967, Mamma Rosa had been informed that "the world is in mud . . . the world is being lost little by little . . . the world is on the threshold of terrible tribulations." In June 1967, she was asked by her vision to "do everything to console the minds as the hour of terrible punishment has struck . . . the warning has sounded. . . . We are already 130 years after La Salette and 50 years after Fatima . . . carry only love and peace in the heart. Then when the terrible moments of darkness come you will have Jesus . . . and you will be strong." In December 1967, Mamma Rose was told by the Madonna that she had been chosen as Christ's messenger because "of all people you are the most ignorant."

Do the seers never foresee a rosy future? There does not seem to be much hope and light in most of the prophets' visions. However, gloomy as he was for the most part, Nostradamus had a sincere and often-stated belief in a Golden Age that was to succeed the holocaust.

This gleam of optimism in the *Centuries* was seized upon by the Nazis during World War II (another event foreseen by the astrologer), and was perverted to their own use. This came about when Goebbels, the Minister of Propaganda, was introduced to Nostradamus' work by his wife, who chose the rhymes nightly as bedtime reading. Goebbels found the verses to his occult taste, and, together with the Gestapo chief, twisted their meanings to announce predictions of a total German victory. In May 1940, the German dropped copies of the altered *Centuries* by air over France to demoralize the populace. The Allies later retaliated by scattering their own version of the rhymes for propaganda purposes over the towns and cities of Germany.

Because Nostradamus deliberately obscured his meanings, his verses lend themselves to greatly different interpretations. His disciples have been accused of something worse than differing interpretations, however. They have been indicted for fitting prophecies to known facts. Many also regard the prophecies themselves as falling within the Theory of Probabilities, which states that if forecasts are sufficient in range and number, some of them must inevitably come true. Whether or not this theory is accepted, Nostradamus' account of the third world war tells of the appearance of Lucifer in the shape of a man, the collapse of the papacy, and the dominance of Communism.

With the razing of Rome, Paris, New York, and London, there will be 27 years of pain and bloodshed while the "King of Horror" deploys his aerial forces to eliminate his "enemies," according to details of the prediction. The red flag will flutter over the ruins of the Vatican, and the hemisphere-to-hemisphere firing of atomic warheads and weapons will ensure that "the universal conflagration shall be preceded by many great inundations, so that there shall scarce be any land that shall not be covered with water. . . . Before and after these inundations in many countries there shall be such scarcity of rain, and such a great deal of fire, and burning stones shall fall from Heaven, that nothing unconsumed shall be left. All this shall happen before the great conflagration.'

However, there is a silver lining in the cloud: all the death, anguish, and havoc is for the ultimate good of mankind. Nostradamus stresses that the disasters and tribulations at the end of the 20th century are necessary in order to prepare the ground for building the ideal world—rather in the way that filthy and decaying slums are demolished to make way for sound new housing. Nostradamus dedicated *Centuries* to his young son, whose "years are too few and months incapable to receive into thy weak understanding what I am forced to define of futurity." In this dedication, the astrologer closes on a note of cheer and optimism with a prediction that the best of all possible worlds will follow the worst.

"After this [the man-made and natural disasters] has lasted a certain time, there will be renewed another reign of Saturn, a truly great and golden age."

Karl Ernst Krafft, a Swiss astrologer living in Germany during World War II, studied and interpreted the obscure prophecies of Nostradamus. His work was taken over by the Propaganda Ministry, and twisted for use in psychological warfare. Krafft was arrested by the Nazis in 1941, and, after periods in and out of prison, died only four years later.

# 8

# The Moderns

Above: Jeane Dixon, America's most famous living clairvoyant, sees things to come through telepathy, revelation, meditation, and dreams. Her prediction of President Kennedy's untimely and violent end made her name a household word from coast to coast.

As she entered St. Matthew's Cathedral in Washington D.C. on a drizzly morning in the fall of 1952, Jeane Dixon felt no immediate premonition of evil. A deeply religious woman, she was, in fact, glowing with anticipation — a feeling that had possessed her for several days. "It was a feeling of expectancy," she explained, "as if something momentous was going to happen, and I would be involved." She moved forward to start her devotions, and stood reverentially before the statue of the Virgin Mary. Then something happened that was to haunt her for the next decade and more.

Right: President Kennedy won the affection and respect of most of his countrymen in the brief period he held office before an assassin's bullet cut him down.

# "This young man would be assassinated"

"... Suddenly the White House appeared before me in dazzling brightness. Coming out of a haze, the numerals 1–9–6–0 formed above the roof. An ominous dark cloud appeared, covering the numbers, and dripped slowly onto the White House ... Then I looked down and saw a young man, tall and blue-eyed, crowned with a shock of thick brown hair, quietly standing in front of the main door.

"I was still staring at him when a voice came out of nowhere, telling me softly that this young man, a Democrat, to be seated as President in 1960, would be assassinated while in office. The vision faded into the wall—into the distance as softly as it had come, but it stayed with me until that day in Dallas when it was fulfilled." That day in Dallas came 11 years later with the assassination of President John F. Kennedy. His funeral mass was said in the very church in which Jeane Dixon had had her vision.

In 1952, Jeane Dixon was 34 years old. At the age of eight in California, she had been taken by her mother to see a gypsy fortune teller. The gypsy lived in a canvas wagon, which she shared with a brood of chickens, and was used to being approached by the local people from Santa Rosa. When she took Jeane's hands in hers and turned them over, however, she dropped her customary mask of impassivity. "This little girl is going to be world famous," she gasped. "She will be able to foresee worldwide changes, because she is blessed with the gift for prophecy. Never have I seen such palm lines!" Several marks on Jean's hand excited the gypsy, who told Jeane's mother of their significance. "They mean that this child will grow mightily in wisdom," she said seriously. "The lines in the left hand are the blueprint of one's dreams and potential. Those in the right hand signify what you do with what God has given you. She is already developing fast." Later, a Hindu mystic said that markings like Jeane's occurred no more than once in a thousand years.

As Jeane grew up, she discovered that her Extra Sensory Perception (ESP) was far in excess of that of most people. Tests showed that her ability was somewhere between 90 and 97 percent, while others were lucky to have a rating of between 3 and 7 percent. Jeane learned astrology from a Jesuit priest at Loyola University in Los Angeles, and though she preferred to give personal readings by means of a crystal ball, she believed it possible to help people through reading the stars. Her popular column, "Jeane Dixon's Horoscope," began to appear in more than 300 newspapers throughout the United States, where it has been estimated that some six million newspaper readers follow the stars each day. She attracted attention at highest social and political levels by her obvious sincerity and desire to do good.

Mrs. Dixon recounts that President Franklin D. Roosevelt summoned her to the White House at the height of World War II late in 1944. He wanted to know how much time he had left in which to complete his "mission for mankind." Mrs. Dixon looked solemnly at the aging President, and asked him if he really wanted to know the truth. He affirmed that he did, and her answer was abrupt. "You have no more than six months," she told him. He died suddenly on April 12, 1945.

By then, Jeane Dixon had taken her place among the leading

Right: deeply devout, Jeane Dixon goes to church early every morning. Here she is shown lighting devotional candles in St. Matthew's, the very church in which she had the vision of John Kennedy's assassination, and in which his funeral mass was said.

Below: Mrs. Dixon told an ill-looking President Roosevelt that he had only six more months to live in late 1944. "I could sense that he had felt a premonition of his own death," she later said.

Above: the bereaved widow and brothers of President John Kennedy march in his funeral procession. Later, Jeane Dixon made a prediction that Robert Kennedy too would be assassinated in the Ambassador Hotel in Los Angeles. Ironically, Mrs. Dixon made her accurate forecast in the very same hotel that was the scene of the killing.

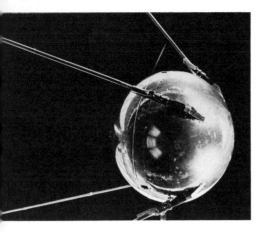

**Above: Sputnik I, the world's first satellite, was successfully launched by the Soviet Union on October 4, 1957. Four years earlier, on a television program, Jeane Dixon had gazed into her crystal, and had described a vision of "a silver ball" going into space.**

seers of the mid-20th century, and she went on to demonstrate that—for her at least—the present and the future were one. She accurately predicted the partition of India, which she saw in her crystal in 1945. At that time, she told an Indian military attaché at a Washington reception that his country would be divided on June 2, 1947. At a party in Washington early in 1945, she told Winston Churchill that he would lose the coming election. He protested crossly that "the people of England will never let me down"; but he was defeated and replaced as prime minister that July. She foresaw the deaths of UN Secretary Dag Hammarskjold and Mahatma Gandhi; the suicide of Marilyn Monroe; the launching of the Soviet space capsule Sputnik 1; and the "uncontrollable blaze" that killed three young astronauts and destroyed an Apollo rocket at Cape Kennedy in 1967.

Like Mother Shipton—the 16th-century English oracle who predicted that the world would end in 1881—Mrs. Dixon has made her mistakes. She was wrong, for instance, when she forecast that China would cause a world war in 1958. She explains this error by the fact that she is a "mere channel of communication," and, although she was shown the correct symbols, she failed to interpret them correctly.

Refusing money except for her writings, Mrs. Dixon makes a habit of giving predictions before sizeable gatherings of people. At a lunch on the roof of the Washington Hotel in 1968, she told her immediate neighbor at the table not to fret about Martin Luther King and his thousands of followers

**Right: astronauts Grissom, White, and Chaffee were the first fatalities of the US space program, killed in a fire that destroyed Apollo 4 on January 27, 1967. A month earlier—during what should have been a happy holiday meeting with a friend—Jeane Dixon had foreseen the tragedy with terrible and exact clarity.**

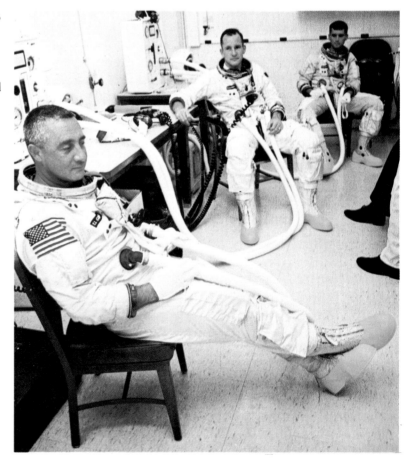

marching on Washington. "Don't you worry about that," she said, with an unexpected sadness in her voice. "Martin Luther King will not get to Washington . . . he will be shot before he can get here. He will be shot in the neck . . . He will be shot first . . . and Robert Kennedy will be next!"

A few days later, the first part of her prophecy came true with the killing of Martin Luther King. On May 28, 1968, Mrs. Dixon felt sure that death was "finally and irrevocably" closing in on Senator Kennedy. She was addressing a convention in the Grand Ballroom of the Ambassador Hotel in Los Angeles, and invited questions from the floor. One woman asked her whether Robert Kennedy would become president, and everyone in the room waited eagerly for the reply. "The answer came to me with a fierce, unrelenting finality," Jeane wrote later. "It came in the form of a black curtain that descended between the audience and me . . . It dropped down like lightning, and did not stop until it had reached the floor. It was black . . . and swift . . . it was final! . . . 'No, he will not. He will never be president of the United States,' I answered calmly, 'because of a tragedy right here in this hotel.'"

The next week Robert Kennedy was due to speak at the Ambassador Hotel, and Mrs. Dixon repeated her warning to an American Legion official and to the mother-in-law of the lieutenant governor of Florida. The official advised her not to upset anyone. The woman, however, made a serious effort to contact the senator's mother about the warning from the

Below: a photograph of the ruined space capsule in which three young astronauts had lost their lives revealed a tool entangled in a mass of wires. Mrs. Dixon had predicted that the capsule had faulty wires, and that some kind of tool would be found "at the trouble site."

"Prophetess of Washington." Her telephone calls were not returned. Early on the morning of June 5, a bullet fired by an assassin ended Robert Kennedy's life at the Ambassador Hotel.

Could the senseless killings of the Kennedy brothers have been averted through Mrs. Dixon's prophetic warnings? Mrs. Dixon herself feels that the younger brother's might have been, but not the president's. She explains this by making a difference between what she learns of the future by "revelation," and what she foresees by "telepathy." In the case of revelation, no power on earth can stop the event revealed. Revelations come rarely to Mrs. Dixon, but her vision of President Kennedy's assassination was one of them. In the case of telepathy, which is an almost continuous part of Mrs. Dixon's daily existence, the outcome can be altered by altering the situation. Because her foreglimpse of Robert Kennedy's killing was by telepathy, it might have been avoided on her warning—perhaps by a change of time or place of the speech.

Although Jeane Dixon's early vision of President John Kennedy's death was particularly detailed, it was not the only precognition of the tragedy. Many people throughout the world —some of them professional seers, most of them average citizens—felt that John Kennedy's doomed future had been revealed to them. One of the warnings came from an Englishman. He wrote to President Kennedy on October 25, 1963, less than a month before the President's death. In his letter, he quoted this passage from an article of his own previously published in *Fate Annual:* "The President may make powerful enemies among his own people, and I would not rule out the possibility of an attempted assassination or worse if he is caught off his guard. There may be a strange turning of the Wheel of Fate, for it is just a century ago since the American Civil War was raging with unabated fury. President Lincoln was shot by a madman in 1865 . . . " He then added directly: "I am deeply concerned for your personal safety, and would respectfully urge you to strengthen your bodyguard, especially when you are in the street and other public places."

If the visions of Jeane Dixon were not always taken seriously in America, seers like her were believed at the highest level in Burma. When the Burmese gained their independence from Great Britain in 1948, their leaders called in astrologers to advise them. Based on the astral calculations they were given, politicians chose the seemingly eccentric hour of 4:20 a.m. on January 4 to launch the new nation. Nine years later, and acting on similar advice, nearby Nepal began its new national life at 4:50 a.m. on June 30. In 1950, the Burmese cabinet resigned because of information they got from astrologers. The new ministers were sworn in less than 24 hours later exactly between 9:15 and 9:20 a.m. "It is then," the fortune tellers told Prime Minister Thakin Nu, "that the stars and planets will most favor our country and bless all that we do."

Another modern clairvoyant whose forecasts received much publicity was Elisabeth Steen. In 1964 she started to have precognitive flashes about the destruction of San Francisco, where she then lived. She had previously predicted the horror of the flood that devastated much of her native Holland in 1952, and

Above: like some dreadful remake of a film, family members gather at the grave of Senator Robert Kennedy, the second brother to fall from an assassin's bullet. Both events had been foreseen by Mrs. Dixon through psychic powers.

Right: no warning vibrations came to Jeane Dixon on Martin Luther King's first great march on Washington in 1957. In 1968, however, she forecast that he would be shot before reaching the capital city.

had also foreseen the death of Martin Luther King—although she was wrong on the date by two days. On the strength of these successes, newspapers reported her every psychic utterance, the late pop singer Mama Cass made a record called "California Earthquake," and the Steen family moved from San Francisco to the state of Washington. According to Elisabeth, the disaster would strike toward the end of March 1969. While thousands of San Franciscans prayed for deliverance at that period—and hundreds of others made a point of being out of town—nothing happened to the city. There was one victim, however, although she no longer lived in California. On March 28, Elisabeth Steen died suddenly in Spokane.

The way in which Mrs. Steen had projected knowledge of her own impending doom onto that of an entire community is not untypical of some of those who get glimpses of our tomorrows today. In the case of a beautiful young actress at the Comédie Française in Paris, however, her intimations of disaster were limited strictly to herself. Mademoiselle Irene Muza frightened her colleagues and friends when, in an hypnotic trance, she wrote down what the future held for her. "My career will be short," she stated. "I dare not say what my end will be: it will be terrible." Before Mlle. Muza came out of her trance, her friends destroyed her written words and swore not to tell her what she had foreseen.

A few months passed. Then one day the actress went to the hairdresser and met her self-predicted terrible end! An assistant accidentally dropped some antiseptic lotion on a lighted stove, and Irene Muza was like a "blazing doll" within seconds. She was rushed to the hospital, but died within hours of severe burns that had left her without skin or hair.

Time and again in recent history, scientists and non-scientists have come up with theories and possible evidence suggesting that, while our memory dwells on the past, part of our thinking and reasoning exist simultaneously in the present and future. The distinguished English astronomer and physicist,

Above: San Francisco was devastated by the big 1906 earthquake. If Elisabeth Steen's vision of a 1969 catastrophe had come true, the more built-up modern city might have suffered even more. Right: this orange grove in California was pushed out of line by the San Andreas fault, which also affects San Francisco. Below: the mild shock that hit San Francisco in 1966 left rubble like this behind. Perhaps this minor quake helped people believe in Mrs. Steen's prediction of a calamity in 1969.

Sir Arthur Eddington, spent much of his career studying the mysteries of time and space. He concluded that it was not time which moved, but we ourselves. "This division into past and future is closely associated with our ideal of causation and freewill," he wrote. "In a perfectly determinate scheme, the past and future may be regarded as lying mapped out—as much available to present exploration as the distant parts of space. Events do not happen, they are just there, and we come across them." He also realized how much humanity was subject to the pull of the universe in all that it thought and did. This belief was echoed by Giorgio Piccardi, head of the Institute for Physical Chemistry at the University of Florence, who declared: "To be subjected to cosmic effects, man does not have to be shot into space; he does not even have to leave his home. Man is always surrounded by the universe, since the universe is everywhere."

At the moment, no modern prophets seem to be able to see a future much beyond the year 2000. Like Nostradamus, many of them feel that the world will have just barely survived and be recovering from a global holocaust at that time. However, on the material level, scientists do not bear out such forebodings. Dr. Herman Kahn, director of the Hudson Institute, has predicted the 100 technical innovations that will have been invented by the year 2000—and they will include "programmed dreams."

Although Jeane Dixon asserts that the years just before 1999 will hold great struggles for humanity, she also believes that we will win through to a better life for all. She bases this belief on the "most significant and soul-stirring" vision of her life, which took place shortly before sunup on February 5, 1962. At 7:17 a.m. on that day, she rose and gazed out of her window in Washington. Her eyes did not meet "the bare-limbed trees of the city," but beheld an "endless desert scene, broiled by a relentless sun." When the sun's rays parted, Mrs. Dixon saw Queen Nefertiti of ancient Egypt hand in hand with her

Jeane Dixon receives hundreds of letters a day, most of them pleading for help. "Vibrations tell me which writers are most sincerely in need of help, and which I can help," Mrs. Dixon has said.

Pharaoh. In her free arm, the Queen cradled a baby in soiled and ragged clothing. The infant was in "stark contrast to the magnificently arrayed royal couple." In her biography of Jeane Dixon, *A Gift of Prophecy*, Ruth Montgomery recounts Mrs. Dixon's interpretation of her dream as follows:

"A child born somewhere in the Middle East shortly after 7 a.m. (EST) on February 5, 1962, will revolutionize the world. Before the close of the century he will bring together all mankind in one all-embracing faith. This will be the foundation of a new Christianity, with every sect and creed united through this man, who will walk among the people to spread the wisdom of the Almighty Power. This person, though born of humble peasant origin, is a descendant of Queen Nefertiti . . . There was nothing kingly about his coming—no kings or shepherds to do homage to this newborn baby—but he is the answer to the prayers of a troubled world. Mankind will begin to feel the

140

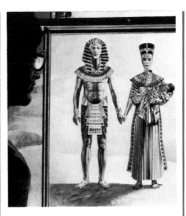

## New Hope for The World

It was a wintry February day in Washington, D.C. in 1962. Jeane Dixon—called "the Prophetess of Washington"—awoke just before sunup, and moved toward her bedroom window facing east. There, instead of the city streets lined with bare trees, she saw a vivid desert scene. Out of the rays of a sun that glowed like a golden ball stepped Queen Nefertiti of ancient Egypt, hand-in-hand with her Pharaoh. She carried a newborn baby, whose ragged clothing jarred the eye compared to the gorgeous raiment of the royal couple. A few minutes later, the baby had grown to manhood. He was surrounded by worshipers of every color, race, and creed—and Jeane Dixon felt herself to be inside the very center of the vision with the adoring crowds.

This, then, was "the most significant and soul-stirring" vision ever experienced by the modern seer, Jeane Dixon. She interprets it as the promise of a great "new Christianity" that will unite all the world as one in peace. The leader will be the baby of her vision. "His power will grow greatly until 1999," she says, "at which time the . . . earth will probably discover the full meaning of the vision."

great force of this man in the early 1980s, and during the subsequent 10 years, the world as we know it will be reshaped and revamped into one without wars or suffering. His power will grow until 1999, at which time, the peoples of this earth will probably discover the full meaning of the vision."

Asked how she felt at the time of her vision, Jeane Dixon answered: "I felt suspended and enfolded, as if I were surrounded by whipped cream. For the first time I understood the full meaning of the Biblical phrase, 'My cup runneth over.' I loved all mankind. I felt that I would never again need food or sleep, because I had experienced perfect peace."

Like her prophetic forerunners, Jeane Dixon has not broken through the time barrier into the 21st century. For that vision—be it of Jeane Dixon's perfect peace, of Nostradamus' golden age after the holocaust, or of an entirely different picture—we must await a new prophet for whom the future is now.

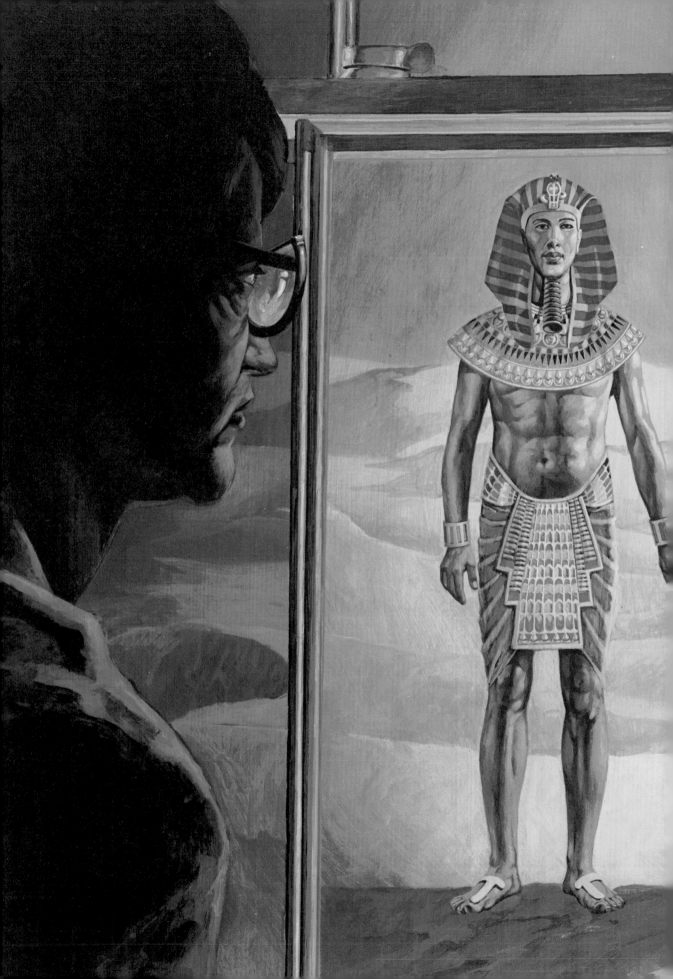

# Picture Credits

2    photo Richard Hatswell © Aldus Books
4    Michael Holford Library photo
7    The Bettmann Archive
8-9    *Illustrated London News*
10-1(T)    National Gallery, London/photo John Freeman © Aldus Books
11(B)    Archiv für Kunst und Geschichte, Berlin
13(T)    *Radio Times* Hulton Picture Library
13(B)    The Estate of J. W. Dunne
14    Anton Lubke, *Die Uhr*, VDI-Verlag, Düsseldorf, 1958
15(TL)    Museum of the History of Science, Oxford/photo Ken Coton © Aldus Books
15(BL)    Michael Holford Library photo
15(R)    reproduced by permission of the Trustees of the British Museum
16    photo David Swann © Aldus Books
18-9    Christopher Foss © Aldus Books
21, 2(T)    *Radio Times* Hulton Picture Library
22(B)    Staatliche Museen für Volkekunde, München
23    Taya Zinkin/photo John Webb © Aldus Books
24(L)    The Museum of the American Indian. Heve Foundation
24(R)    Smithsonian Institution, Washington, D.C.
25    Aldus Archives
26-7    Gino D'Achille © Aldus Books
28, 9(T) (C)    Josef Muench
29(B)    The Hamlyn Group Picture Library
31(TL)    photo Peter Clayton
31(TR)    © Commander Gatti Expeditions
31(B)    photo Richard Hatswell © Aldus Books
32(T)    Mansell Collection
32(B), 33(T)    Mary Evans Picture Library
33(C)    Mansell Collection
33(B)    The Hamlyn Group Picture Library
34(T)    The Bettmann Archive
34(B)    *Radio Times* Hulton Picture Library
35(TL)    Gianni Roghi/Camera Press
35(TR)    Mary Evans Picture Library
35(B), 36    Mansell Collection
37(T)    Theodore Donaldson/FPG
37(B)    Steve Shapiro/Black Star, New York
38    photo Fred Gettings
39    reproduced by permission of the Trustees of the British Museum
40    Musée Guimet, Paris
41(T)    Kim Young Eun/Bavaria-Verlag
41(B)    *Radio Times* Hulton Picture Library
42(T)    photo Malcolm Scoular © Marshall Cavendish Ltd.
42-3(B)    Aldus Archives
43(T)    Keystone, Tokyo
44(T)    photo Peter Clayton
44(B)    Mansell Collection
45(T)    Uffizi Gallery, Florence/photo G. B. Pineider
45(B)    Mansell Collection
46(L)    Staatliche Museen, Berlin
46(R)    The MacQuitty International Collection

47    City of Manchester Art Galleries
48(T)    British Museum/Photo David Swann © Aldus Books
48(B)    *Radio Times* Hulton Picture Library
49(R)    Rudoux et Vaucouleurs, *L'Astronomie*, Editions Flammarion, Paris
50(T)    British Museum/photo David Swann © Aldus Books
50(B)    Aldus Archives
51    Mary Evans Picture Library
52-3(T)    photo Marvin Lichtner/Camera Press
52-3(B)    Süddeutscher Verlag, München
54    photo Marvin Lichtner/Camera Press
55    Mary Evans Picture Library
56(L)    Cheiro, *You and Your Hand*, Jarrold & Sons, Ltd., 1932
57    *Illustrated London News*
58-9    Cheiro, *You and Your Hand*, Jarrold & Sons, Ltd., 1932
60-1    photo Richard Hatswell © Aldus Books
62(B)    Mary Evans Picture Library
63(T)    Snark International
63(B)    photo Rominger/Camera Press
64    Aldus Archives
65    *Radio Times* Hulton Picture Library
66    Courtesy Peter Jackson
67(R)    Aldus Archives
68    Mansell Collection
69(L)    Mary Evans Picture Library
69(R)    Mansell Collection
70    The Hamlyn Group Picture Library
71    Aldus Archives
72(L)    *Radio Times* Hulton Picture Library
72(R), 73    Cheiro, *You and Your Hand*, Jarrold & Sons, Ltd., 1932
74    photo Marvin Lichtner/Camera Press
75    Michael Holford Library photo
76-7(B)    Keystone
77(T)    Waddingtons Playing Card Co. Ltd.
78-9(T)    Tarot deck printed by courtesy of U.S. Games Systems, Inc., New York and A. G. Müller et Cie. Ordinary deck, Waddingtons Playing Card Co. Ltd.
78(B)    Mary Evans Picture Library
79(B)    Victor Englebert/Susan Griggs
80(L), 81    Aldus Archives
80(R)    published by Rider & Company, London
82    Snark International
83(TL)    reprinted by courtesy of U.S. Games Systems, Inc., New York and A. G. Müller et Cie
83(TC)    courtesy J. M. Simon
83(TR)    published by Rider & Company, London
83(BL)    courtesy Samuel Weiser, Inc. and Llewellyn Publications, Inc.
83(BR)    one card from the James Bond deck by Fergus Hall reprinted by permission of U.S. Games Systems, Inc., Eon Productions Ltd. and Glidrose Publications Limited
84(T)    Snark International
85(T)    Mary Evans Picture Library
85(B)    *Radio Times* Hulton Picture Library
86-7    reprinted by courtesy of U.S. Games Systems, Inc., New York and A. G. Müller et Cie
88(T)    photo Richard Hatswell © Aldus

Books
88-9(B)    reprinted by courtesy of U.S. Games Systems, Inc., New York and A. G. Müller et Cie
90(T)    photo Richard Hatswell © Aldus Books
90(B), 91    reprinted by courtesy of U.S. Games Systems, Inc., New York and A. G. Müller et Cie
92(T)    photo Richard Hatswell © Aldus Books
92(B), 93    reprinted by courtesy of U.S. Games Systems, Inc., New York and A. G. Müller et Cie
94    photo Marvin Lichtner/Camera Press
95    *The Sunday Times*
98-9    Bruno Elettori © Aldus Books
100(L)    *Daily Telegraph* Colour Library
100(R)    Colour Library International
101    Picturepoint, London
102(T)    *Radio Times* Hulton Picture Library
102(B)    Mansell Collection
103    photo Mike Busselle © Aldus Books
104(L)    Süddeutscher Verlag, München
104(TR)    *Radio Times* Hulton Picture Library
104(B)    after Sigmund Freud, *The Interpretation of Dreams*
106(L)    Bibliothèque Nationale, Paris
106(R)    British Museum/photo John Freeman © Aldus Books
107    Mansell Collection
108(T)    *Radio Times* Hulton Picture Library
108(B)    Aldus Archives
109(B)    *Radio Times* Hulton Picture Library
110-1    Gino D'Achille © Aldus Books
112-3(T)    photos Mike Busselle © Aldus Books
113(B)    Mansell Collection
114    Aldus Archives
115    Snark International
116    The Bettmann Archive
117    Mansell Collection
118-9    The Tate Gallery, London
120(T)    Popperfoto
120(B)    The Bettmann Archive
121    Mansell Collection
122(B)    City of Birmingham Museums and Art Gallery
123    reproduced by kind permission of Lord Primrose, Earl of Rosebery
124    *Psychic News*
126-7    Christopher Foss © Aldus Books
128(T)    Pictorial Press, London
128(B)    Aldus Archives
129    David Paramor Collection, London
130    photo Rudolfo Bertorelli/Camera Press
131    *Life* © Time Inc.
133(T)    photo Rudolfo Bertorelli/Camera Press
133(BL)    Imperial War Museum, London
133(BR)    Henri Dauman/Colorific!
134(T)    Fotohronika Tass;
134(B)    United States Information Service, London
135    NASA
137(T)    Rex Features
137(B)    The John Hillelson Agency
138-9(T)    *Illustrated London News*
139(C)    photo by John S. Shelton
139(B)    Gene Daniels/Transworld Features
140    photo Rudolfo Bertorelli/Camera Press
142-3    Bruno Elettori © Aldus Books